90 DAYS FOR LIFE

*"Look among the nations! Observe! Be astonished!
Wonder! Because I am doing something in your
days—You would not believe if you were told."*

Habakkuk 1:5 (NASV)

Fred Kim
Ps. 96:2

90 DAYS FOR LIFE

by

Fred Kerr

Hannibal Books
Hannibal, Missouri—"America's Home Town"
(Use coupon in back to order extra copies of this and
other helpful books.)

Dedicated to my precious wife Mary who walked through this adventure with me in her special, wonderful way.

What others Say About
90 Days For Life

Adrian Rogers, pastor and former president of the Southern Baptist Convention: *"90 Days For Life will cause any sensitive person to do some hard thinking. It is a gripping story that sounds as if it came straight out of the Book of Acts. Don't miss reading it."*

John W. Alexander, President Emeritus, InterVarsity Christian Fellowship: *"Fred Kerr's 90 Days For Life is a fascinating and sobering account of how it feels to be arrested and sent to jail for one's religious convictions. I worked with Fred for several years when we were staff members with Inter-Varsity Christian Fellowship, and I know him to be a committed follower of the Lord Jesus Christ, willing to suffer for his Savour's name."*

Dr. J. Robert McQuilkin, President, Columbia Bible College and Seminary: *"A fascinating story I did not want to put down. I came away from Fred Kerr's gripping story of 90 Days For Life with—*
—An intimate glimpse of the inside of one of America's most famous jails...
—A better appreciation of the intense commitment on the part of many who participate in Operation Rescue...
—Admiration for one man's Christlike spirit...and a rising indignation that our nation is behaving the way it is...
—Conviction of failure to be the kind of evangelistic witness I should be, along with inspiration and amazement at the unending creativity of Fred's witness...
—Awe at the majestic power of God in behalf of His people...
—All of this came my way with no pressure or preaching, just an exciting, well-written story of God's grace in the life of my friend, Fred Kerr. You won't regret the time spent with Fred in Fulton County Jail!"

Michael Hirsh, Atlanta Director of Operation Rescue: *"Fred Kerr's account in 90 Days For Life is an encouragement to all those who want to end child killing. His example is one we all should follow. . . ."*

Contents

Preface

This book is based primarily on the journal, recollections and other notes which I kept during my incarceration in Atlanta's Fulton County Jail.

It is not written for the purpose of addressing the legal issues or people related to my being in jail. Nor is it written to pass judgment on the legal innocence or guilt of any inmate with whom I was associated while in jail. The names of all inmates have been changed to protect both the innocent and the guilty.

This book is really two stories woven together. The first one is what a wonderful God did inside the jail. Ministry opportunites should follow Jesus' disciples wherever they go. This story is offered in love to those who have interest in spiritual things.

The second story is that of a pro-lifer's experience. But it's not just my story, it's one that others could tell and with more reason. I think of it as our story. Many have paid, or are still paying a price, to stand for the unborn.

This includes prayer warriors, rescuers, homemakers, sidewalk counselors, attorneys, leaders, office workers, picketers, lobbyists, volunteers, legislators, speakers, doctors, phone callers, supporters, et al. I suspect that a variety of pro-lifers can identify with various conversations or experiences which I had inside the jail.

Together, many Americans holding traditional family values feel the grief, anguish, and the frustration that this heartless child killing brings. Together we hurt for the helpless unborn as they daily have arms and legs jerked off. We reach out to the often forgotten, long term suffering of the post-aborted mothers.

Together, we experienced disappointment in a weak Supreme Court that after two centuries of safety has allowed the womb to become a killing field.

Though baby killing is not a proud chapter in our country's history it is surely a true one. It's a story that needs to be told and remembered.

So for any pro-lifers who choose to claim it in part or whole, this is their story too.

Chapter 1

"Sentenced for the Unborn"

Friday evening, July 29, 1988. My wife Mary and I were talking with friends in the living room of our South Carolina home. We happened to turn on the TV just in time to catch part of a newscast on a Christian station that showed Operation Rescue in action. What I saw stirred me to the depths of my being. Here was a non-violent way to actually save lives.

There, right before my eyes, Christian believers were putting their bodies between unborn babies and abortionists, while sidewalk counselors pleaded with the mothers. Some mothers actually turned away to return home and await the birth of their child or to seek counsel in a crisis pregnancy center. Their babies had been saved just short of the death chambers. There was just one problem: some rescuers were arrested and charged with breaking the law.

I had long grieved over the murder of over a million-and-a-half babies a year in the United States. I hurt for these little ones, knowing every one was precious to the Saviour. I wanted to do something more than pray, lament the carnage to friends, and appear at the annual rally in January to mark another sad anniversary of the infamous Roe v. Wade Supreme Court decision. Above all, I yearned for the day when the killing would stop. But despite all the rallies and statements, the killing had continued.

My eyes glued to the screen, I heard the narrator announce that another "rescue" was planned for Atlanta in a few days. A challenging thought hit me: I could easily drive to Atlanta down I-20 in four hours. I could be a rescuer. I could join the intervention.

Sleep did not come well that night as I wrestled with the implications of participation. It would mean civil disobedience and possible arrest. I might even be put in jail.

I thought of the civil rights demonstrations that aroused the nation's conscience in the 1960's. Laws that outlawed segregation and discrimination were passed. Laws which most Americans came to accept.

There was one big difference between the victims of racism and of abortion. Racism denied blacks their constitutional rights, forcing them to become second class citizens. Abortion—the civil rights issue of the 80's—denied innocent, pre-born babies the ultimate civil right, the right to live.

Would civil rights have been won for blacks without brave people putting their freedom on the line? Probably not, I decided. Would the killing of babies now be stopped without the same thing happening? I didn't want to know.

Surely, I rationalized, abortion can be halted without mass civil disobedience. Surely, the Supreme Court will reverse Roe v. Wade. Or Congress will pass a law. Or the states will ratify a Human Life Amendment to the Constitution to stop the killings.

"Lord, let others rescue if they want. But why me? Why can't I continue to take a stand without risking arrest and jail.?"

I slept and awoke to a new day. I hoped my new concern would pass, as news of some earthquake halfway around the globe has a way of doing. But God would not let me off the hook so easily. It wasn't "a" problem. It had become "my" problem—my big challenge.

I struggled. I agonized. I had no peace in my spirit as I "arm wrestled" with God.

The Lord came straight out with me. *"You can go to Atlanta and help save the lives of some babies who will otherwise die before laws are changed. So what if you are arrested and sent to jail. I went to the cross for you."*

"But, Lord, if I'm arrested, how will Mary and I—faith missionaries—pay the fine? I've never been to jail, except to preach and minister. When I'm finished, the jailer always let me out. This 'visit' could last for months, maybe even years. What will happen to our student ministry? Can Mary carry on alone with me in jail? And what if I'm attacked by some pervert. I'm not the strongest person in the world, you know."

All my "what ifs" were of no avail. At some point during the next two days God led me across my personal Rubicon. Jesus had come all the way from Heaven to save me from eternal death. All I had to do was go to Atlanta and help save some babies from being murdered. And if arrest and jailing resulted, well, that would be new ground to walk on.

"Lord, I can't make it by myself. Jesus, You'll have to supply the grace and courage for whatever comes."

That same day I talked to Mary about the decision. She was open to going with me. I told her, "Sweetheart, I'd rather you keep the home fires burning."

Tuesday afternoon, August 2, I drove over to Atlanta. Rescues and arrests had been in the news daily since the Democratic National Convention just two weeks before. Spurred by the publicity, rescuers had continued pouring in from all over the country. Local police had maintained surveillance of the pro-life rallies and rescues.

That evening I attended a rally of two to three hundred pro-life people at which Randall Terry, the founder of "Operation Rescue," shared some of the beginnings of the movement.*

Randall told us that just four years before he and his wife, Cindy, began standing outside abortion mills in Binghamton, New York, pleading with expectant mothers to choose life for their unborn children. After some discouraging events they were joined by 30 pro-lifers from their church. Their combined effort resulted in five pregnant women turning away from that clinic. Five babies were saved from the abortionist that year.

The next year Randall and six others launched the first rescue mission. They went to the abortion clinic just before the mothers were due to arrive and locked themselves in an inner room. When the police came, they went limp and had to be carried and dragged out of the building. Charged with criminal trespass and resisting arrest, all seven were tried, found guilty, and fined $60. The six who had joined Randall chose to pay the $60. Randall refused and went to jail.

More interventions and jail terms followed as more rescues on behalf of the unborn were attempted. In 1986, 106 were arrested in St. Louis alone. The next year almost 300 rescuers sealed off access to an abortuary in New Jersey. No babies were slaughtered there that day. The police held off for several hours, then began making arrests.

The movement continued. In May, just three months before we gathered in Atlanta, 10 Protestant pastors, 15 Catholic priests, two monsignors, an auxiliary bishop, four nuns, an Orthodox priest, and even two rabbis joined Operation Rescue in a New York City effort. The next big effort was scheduled for Atlanta.

"We've come here to rescue more precious babies," Randall said.

---

*   The full story of Operation Rescue is told by Randall in his new book by that name, published by Whitaker House, Springdale, PA, 1988.

"We hope all of you will join us."

Several others spoke. The singing, worship, and testimonies were warm, moving, and inspiring. Because the Atlanta operation had been going on for several days, we could pretty well know what to expect.

"If arrested," Operation Rescue leaders advised us, "you will be taken to the Pre-Trial Center and formally charged, photographed, and fingerprinted. If you use the Baby John Doe and Baby Jane Doe aliases, you'll be identifying with the helplessness of the unborn victims."

The next morning, Wednesday, August 3, we had "air cover" when we congregated at a local motel. A police helicopter hovered above as the vans of rescuers, picketers, and sidewalk counselors headed out to the abortuary. The location was kept confidential until the vehicles began their journey.

Driving into the central city, my van carrying 13 rescuers was filled with excitement and tension. It was almost like we were on a landing barge on D-Day, loaded with soldiers preparing to assault Omaha Beach. Except that we had no weapons other than the Sword of the Spirit and prayers to our mighty God.

The 13 came from nine states and included a young expectant couple from Alaska. The wife was six months pregnant. Each sheltered his or her own private thoughts as the van hummed along the expressway. This was no sightseeing trip, but a mission of mercy. We were not in Atlanta to see Stone Mountain but to stand for God in attempting to move an unholy mountain of death. While all this was scary, I held no doubts that we were on a right course. For me it was a time for just clinging to the Lord.

We sat at the entrance of the abortuary singing "Jesus Loves the Little Children" and other hymns. Dozens of picketers walked up and down and around us. Sidewalk counselors were on hand to talk to any mothers who would listen.

The police arrived. They began arresting us one by one. We went limp and had to be carried individually to the paddy wagon. The officers were deliberate and professional in manner.

We sang all the way to the Pre-Trial Center. We felt joy, purpose, and peace.

Once there, we spent hours moving from one holding cell to another, filling out forms and being photographed and fingerprinted, as we were processed in. The officers were again professional and some were even cordial. None appeared disturbed or shocked by our arrival. At the sight of our appearance one officer said, "I believe in what you are doing."

We said "thank you" at every opportunity and tried to be model prisoners. A Christian on a mission of conscience for Jesus wants his attitudes and deeds to be in harmony with His Lord's.

The jails were filled already. Finally they took us into an upper floor gymnasium and gave each of us a thin, grey, vinyl mattress and pillow from bedding stacked against the wall. Here we would eat, sleep, and live, men on one side of the gym, women on the other. Everyone used the gym's only bathroom. It had one sink and commode. The women got their own shower facilities rather quickly. We men didn't get razors and showers until the third day. By then we looked pretty grubby. After most of us men had gone three days without showers or shaves, the rest were probably thankful the gym was as large as it was.

After a couple of days some 30 new rescuers joined us. What a blessing to meet more keyed-up Baby Does who had come to Atlanta from Pennsylvania, Florida, and Colorado to help stop the killing in Atlanta. Several pastors were among them.

God gave us a spiritual retreat. Morning and afternoon we stood in a big circle and had a rousing prayer and praise service. The gym shook with the power, intensity, and sweetness of the worship of God's people. This was the front lines, the cutting edge. It was like having arrived at a cherished destination after a long, long journey.

One afternoon a brother began walking briskly around the gym for exercise. A second person joined in, then a third. In no time people were rising from all over the gym to join the walk. A brother led out in a praise song. The rest picked up the words and melody. It was like God's people marching around Jericho, except that the only trumpets we had were our voices.

An officer strolled in to check on the commotion. He stood and watched for a minute, scratching his head. I'm sure he had never seen or heard prisoners like us. After awhile he left quietly.

We took turns going out in the hall to use the phone which was located next to a row of individual cells that housed more typical inmates. I got to talk to a couple of these fellows. Both prayed to receive Jesus as their Savior. No doubt our singing and praise had already softened their hearts.

Baby Does were scattered all about the gym. Some shared testimonies of what their pro-life organizations were doing back home. A few napped, others read their Bibles or a book. Occasionally a group would cluster for prayer.

The people in the group looked like the ordinary kind of folks you meet in church. But one lady—a pro-life homemaker from up north—shared informally that for the second time in her life she had seen angels.

Angels? Having gone some 50 years myself without seeing any angels, I was curious. "Where are they?"

"There's one right up there," she promptly replied, pointing high up the wall of the gym.

"How tall are they?" I pursued.

"About ten feet," she replied matter-of-factly.

"What color are they?"

"Bronze."

"What are they wearing?"

"The Biblical type outfit with straps up the leg."

Perhaps angels were there—although I never saw any visually—praising God as some of us witnessed to the prisoners in the cells near the hall phone. I thought of what Jesus said: "There is joy in the presence of the angels of God over one sinner that repents" (Luke 15:10).

After four or five days (you kinda lose count of time in confinement), we were bused out to the county farm. There they separated the men from the women, taking the husband who had been in my van from his pregnant wife.

They put the men into a barracks building. The women were housed with regular, female inmates. All of us changed into blue, two piece jail uniforms.

This was a "Hilton" compared to the gym. We had real beds. We could shower freely. The food was even better. We could play football and jog for an hour each day in an exercise yard. They evidently considered us too transient for regular work assignments.

At the county farm we found favor in the sight of God and man. We witnessed to the trustees who brought our food as well as to those who came to sweep our floors. I was strengthened and uplifted in the fellowship and praise sessions held three times a day. The week became the spiritual highlight of my year. Praise be to His glorious Name! He indeed is high and exalted above all powers, peoples, gods, and kings. Hallelujah!

The 70 or so regular inmates in a male barracks across the hall could hear our vibrant singing and praise. We were put in with these "regular" prisoners on our final night at the farm. Kneeling on my bunk I prayed with four or five to receive Christ. Other Baby John Does also won precious souls.

Our "retreat" ended August 10th. All except two of us gave our legal names and were released on personal signature bonds. We could go home until trial. I had been in custody exactly seven days. It would be good to be with my Mary again. We did not know what the upcoming months would bring us. In January we learned that we could avoid trial by exercising a nolo contendere option, pay a $500 fine, and receive restrictions. Or we could go to trial on January 31.

I returned to my ministry in South Carolina and re-entered "normal life." The dawning of the new year brought the realization that I must soon decide about a future course of action. Should I exercise the option, pay the $500 fine, and accept the restrictions of the court? Or should I go to trial? Still unaware of what God would have me to do, Mary and I returned to Atlanta on Monday afternoon, January 30.

That evening we joined other rescuers for discussion and advice on alternatives. During the meeting I felt the need to be alone with God before making my decision. I left Mary and walked outside to do some more arm wrestling with God.

"Lord, I don't want to do this. I don't want to go back to jail." That still, small voice—the voice of God's Holy Spirit—kept telling me, *"Others have gone to jail for obeying a higher law, for standing against the killing. You have the opportunity to give a testimony. I will take care of you. I will see you through."*

Around and around the neighborhood I walked. My feelings or God's will? My way or God's way? Will I let emotion and fear be in the driver's seat or will I submit to the will of God? Can I give it a good shot for the kids, the unborn, who will die unless rescuers stand in the "gap?"

It was fish or cut bait and God wanted me to fish. I surrendered.

"God, this means trusting You in a new and deeper way. I mean really trusting You and doing Your will. I know that to miss it here could mean to miss it big. Jesus, I just want You to be proud of me . . . when Your glory is revealed."

I returned to the meeting.

Eleven of my group of 13 had evidently decided on actions that would keep them from going to trial in Georgia. Some had apparently chosen to exercise the nolo contendere option, pay a $500 fine, and receive restrictions. Others had apparently opted to go home and not return to Georgia for trial.

That left Brenda Roberts and me. Brenda said she would go to trial and defend herself.

I heard my voice—that I believed was in tune with God's will— saying the same. Brenda and I would not take the nolo contendere option.

"Lord, I'm trusting You. Lord, be my shield."

With the coming of morning, God gave me another promise: "Wait on the Lord: be of good courage, and He shall strengthen thine heart: wait, I say, on the Lord" (Psalm 27:14).

We met at the state court building with friends and family and clustered in a prayer circle outside the courtroom before mine and Brenda's trials were to begin. Brenda's husband, Paul, was there to stand resolutely with his wife, as was my ever-present Mary to stand by me.

"Lord, we will accept whatever decision is handed down as from You."

It was time for court to begin. We entered the courtroom when called by the officer. Brenda and I took our seats at the defendants' table. The prosecution was to our right. Our friends sat behind us in the spectators' section.

Both sides looked over the prospective jurors and selected a total of six to hear the case. I don't know why a full twelve were not utilized as elsewhere. Going pro se, or acting as our own attorneys, we were doubly walking by faith today.

Video tapes of the pro-life demonstrations were offered by the prosecution. Much time by the prosecution was devoted to verify that we were indeed at the scene of the incident of August 3. A policeman testified.

I wanted to pursue our motives for being there. What prompted our behavior? I was frustrated at not being able to make points key to our defense.

Finally came the summations. In mine I implored the jury to consider the larger issues at stake here. My words went along this line: "We have larger fish to fry. The soul of the nation is on trial here, more than two people. Will baby killing continue to be legalized and ignored? What kind of society do you want your children and grandchildren to grow up in? What direction do you want our nation to take?

"I ask you to look at our motives in standing up for the babies. Why would a minister with plenty to do in South Carolina come over to Georgia? Brenda and I have nothing to gain from this socially or financially. We're not here for drinking, robbing, or doing drugs. Why did we do this?

"In other trials we often hear the word 'motive' used. Why not today?"

An older lady juror seemed to be deeply feeling my words. Was she with me? Did she too really grasp the national issues at stake? If so, would she stand her ground with the other jurors? We needed only one vote for acquittal.

I spoke of Martin Luther King, Jr.'s regard for human rights. I looked the jurors straight in the eye.

"True greatness includes graciousness and generosity. Shouldn't that encompass giving the benefit of the doubt to those who put themselves out to help others?"

The lady judge gaveled the court into recess. The expressionless jurors retired to consider their verdict. Mary and I and the others walked out into the corridor. I paced and prayed some by myself part of the time. Mary had commented that she would go to her parents' home for a while if I should be sent to jail.

I reflected on the previous year's events in Atlanta. I recalled that peaceful rescues began in Atlanta during the Democratic National Convention in July, 1988. Exactly 1,268 "Baby John and Jane Does" were arrested in Atlanta between July 19 and October 29, 1988. During the summer around 100 of them opted to remain in jail together for weeks on end rather than give their real names. On October 4, 343 were arrested. Forty-one more were arrested on October 29. A few men chose to remain in jail indefinitely rather than give their real names. They were finally released without trial or explanation after serving 100 days as Baby Does. Few of the 1,268 rescuers had come to trial by January, 1989, when we did.

A reporter from **The Atlanta Journal and Constitution**, Lorri Denise Booker, stopped Mary and me, individually, in the hall for comments. She asked me, "Aren't you concerned about your reputation if you go to jail?"

I replied, "Jeremiah the prophet, the apostle Paul, and John the Baptist were put in jail too. That's pretty good company."

The court reconvened. Brenda and I returned to the defendants' section, our loved ones took their seats. The jury returned.

"Ladies and gentlemen, have you reached your verdict?"

"We have, Your Honor. We find Brenda Roberts guilty on all counts. We find Fred Kerr guilty on all counts."

The high ceilinged court room loomed larger as we approached the tall, wooden bench for sentencing. Brenda resolutely stood on my right. To her right was the state's attorney. The impassive deputies hung behind us, ready to respond as ordered. Friends and family in the back of the room appeared to fade as questions were asked of us. I made the point that what hadn't been brought out was that we were acting on our religious convictions. I asked for mercy as this was our first offense. Prior to this we had managed to stay out of jail, except for the week's pre-trial confinement, me for 50 years and Brenda, no doubt, for a long while too.

The prosecutor recommended to the judge one year sentences for us in the state prison.

Finally sentencing began. The judge's pronouncement struck like a thunderbolt: four one-year sentences! It was all suspended but 60 days. I could be released in 30, on condition that I pay a $1760 fine and maintain a 100-yards distance from area abortion facilities.

Brenda received three one-year sentences, all suspended but 60 days, to serve 30, if a $1360 fine was paid, plus the 100 yards restriction.

This—for a first time, misdemeanor charge?

"Sentence begins today," the judge announced. Court was dismissed.

The deputies moved up to escort us to jail. My eyes caught Mary's across the court room. No opportunity for even a parting hug.

Mary told me later how she felt: "I was angry that the world system had won. Yet I also felt the sure conviction that God was in control."

"Unreasonableness may appear to have won the day," I thought, "but God's ways are above ours. His reasons for allowing this are as yet a mystery to me. Mary and I will now have to shift into another gear. Our lives will not be the same as before. I am no longer a free man. Trusting the Lord must take on a deeper meaning."

Brenda and I were rushed downstairs by the officers. I was still keyed up from the excitement of the day. Trusting the Lord was taking on deeper meaning by the hour.

Still numb, we were taken by officers to the Fulton County Jail on Jefferson Street in Atlanta. A variety of feelings and attitudes competed for hearing in my mind. I still had the peace of the Lord. I had no second thoughts about my decision to see this through. I could only keep pressing on in faith.

This would be different than before. I had figured to be in the Pre-trial Center only a day or two, although my stay actually turned out to be a week. Now I would have to serve a much longer time and be housed, not with pro-lifers, but with men from the general prison population.

Chapter 2

"Firstfruits"

Tuesday, January 31.

Within two hours after our trial ended Brenda and I were driven from the courthouse to the jail on Jefferson Street. Brenda was taken to a holding cell for women, I to a similar cell for men.

The spiritually oriented talk and prayer with friends of recent hours was exchanged for questions from officers as I was moved from one holding cell to another.

"Do you have any money to turn in? It can be used to pay for commissary purchases."

"Give me your right thumb for a print." Etc., etc., etc.

Holding cells are big and crowded and devoid of charm, although the expected form of creative "art" adorns the walls. Concrete benches along the walls and a flapless commode are the only furniture. This big cage deep in the bowels of the jail complex is devoid of any breezes drifting through a window. The air is tight and stale.

God is truly giving me peace. I feel no fear for physical safety, though there are all types of fellows in here. I seem to be the only one to have dressed formally for the occasion. With my sport coat, tie, Bible, overnight bag, and writing tablet, I stand out in this big barracks-like room among some 60 "guests" of Georgia taxpayers. This is a new experience for me, a middle-aged evangelist. I must keep notes on what takes place.

A husky fellow with a joyless face looked at me. "Hey, Pal, what'er ya in f'er?"

"For peacefully demonstrating in front of an abortion facility. Have you heard anything about it in the news?"

"Ye'r one of them Baby Does?"

"Yes I am." I pulled out a picture of an aborted baby that plainly showed tiny dismembered head, arms, and feet.

The big guy took one peek and leaned back as if he had been hit in the gut. Several other prisoners crowded around. I had the attention of all in the crowded jail barracks now.

"That's what a tiny innocent baby looks like after the abortionist is through," I said.

A kid of about 22, sitting on the floor, spoke from where all could hear. "You're in jail for demonstrating against that? Nothing else?" The kid looked at me and winced. "You're right to be doing this."

"Yeah," another encouraging voice said, "Somebody's got to protest the killings."

The ice broken, I began moving among the prisoners, asking, "Would you like something to read?" I reached down into my pockets and pulled out some gospel tracts. I selectively offered them to a handful of fellows who appeared interested. One fellow saw me handing them out and asked for one. Not one was refused. What an opportunity to witness. This was better than speaking in a church where anyone can get up and leave if they wish. Hallelujah!

I sat back down on the hard concrete bench and looked around. They were reading the literature.

"Lord, open their eyes. Show them that you love them and will forgive their sins."

Later, one of the younger prisoners approached me, holding one of the tracts, which he had been reading.

"I'm interested in coming to the Lord."

Three other young men gravitated to our bench and joined us.

I addressed my little congregation. "Do you know which way you would go if you should die tonight?"

"Well, I hope I will go to heaven," one drawled.

I looked at first one, then another. "Do you know many who are hoping to go to hell? Everybody is hoping to go to heaven. Are you one hundred percent certain?"

The boy who had initiated the conversation solemnly shook his head. The young man next to him wasn't certain either. The two others said the same.

It was time to get down to business.

"Well, I know for sure where I'd go if I died tonight. You can too. Would you like that?"

They all nodded "yes."

I put my Bible on my knees and turned to Romans 3:23: "'For all have sinned, and come short of the glory of God.'"

"'All,' fellows, means everybody. Those in jail and out. The one who says he hasn't sinned is either a liar or only fooling himself.

"God is holy and just and pure. That's why no unforgiven sinner can enter God's family. God's justice demands that there be a penalty for sin." I read Romans 6:23: "'For the wages of sin is death; but the gift of God is eternal life through Jesus Christ our Lord.' That's spiritual death, eternal death," I explained. "None of us can ever be good enough to go to heaven. Only by the mercy of God can any of us enter there. God's Word says, 'Not by works of righteousness which we have done, but according to His mercy He saved us . . . .'" (Titus 3:5).

The wrinkled brows told me they still weren't clear about not being saved by works, so I pursued the point. "Have you ever seen eggs being made into an omelet?" Heads nodded assent.

I went through the motions of breaking eggs and mixing them in a bowl. "Now suppose by mistake you got some bad eggs mixed in with the good eggs in your omelet. Have you ever smelled any rotten eggs?"

Yes, they had.

"Would you still eat that omelet? Or would you serve it to your guests?"

Heads slowly shook.

I asked, "Why not? What have the bad eggs done?"

"'Messed up the good ones," they agreed in unison.

"My life is like that omelet," I explained. "The bad in my life has messed up any good. I can't offer up my life to God as a pleasing offering to Him. My good works won't cancel out the bad ones. And even worse, my heart is evil. God's Word says, 'The heart is deceitful above all things, and desperately wicked: who can know it?'" (Jeremiah 17:9).

Finally, they seemed to grasp sin's cancerous corruption of each person's nature. I had a very attentive audience. I now told them about God sending His only Son as a love gift for their salvation. I read to them about Jesus dying on the cross to pay for every sin.

"You must ask Jesus to come into your heart, forgive your sins, and sit on the throne of your lives. Do you want to do that? Do you want to do it now?"

All four nodded and knelt on the rough concrete bench. I urged my new friends to pray and they did: "Lord, I'm a sinner. Come into my heart. Forgive me. I believe You died on the cross to wash away every sin I've ever committed. Give me a new heart. Sit on the throne of my life. I want to be saved. I want to go to heaven. Thank You for eternal life."

Later I had a private prayer time of my own: *"Praise God! Thank you, Lord. Jails may lock the body in but they cannot keep Your Spirit out. Glory be to your name. Lord, is this why You brought me here? It must be. What a wonderful way for You to tell me that I am where I am supposed to be for now!"*

The Spirit brought Psalm 27:14 to my mind again: "Wait on the Lord: be of good courage, and He shall strengthen thine heart: wait, I say, on the Lord."

"Thank You, Lord. I really needed that."

Sometime later in the night an overworked trustee, who was now processing all of us in, called out, "Take off all your street clothes." He hurriedly inventoried my clothing, overnight bag, and contents. I held on to a plastic sack which I had stuffed with tracts. I kept my precious study Bible with its wealth of personal notes.

It was time to get one of the standard uniforms being handed out. "Small, medium, or large?" the trustee asked. I opted for the stylish, deep blue, medium, two piece outfit. It's a scrub suit. And I can already observe that it is going to be in fashion this season.

Some of us were taken to yet another holding cell for the balance of the night. Loaded down with vinyl mattress, pillow, and sack, I had to walk some distance. It was holding cell number four for me that night.

It felt good to be some place where I could lie down as well as sleep, even if I did have to sleep on the floor. Sweet sleep. Sweet peace of God which "passes all understanding."

I tried to snatch some sleep despite the noise that almost never ceased. Echoing through the bars from across the hall, I kept hearing two loud inmates having one of those middle-of-the-night, desperate-for-a-topic conversations: "Can elephants do this or that? I'd really like to find out," the voice said. I drifted off.

Wednesday, February 1.

After six a.m. breakfast an officer came to screen us. He asked, "Do you have any diseases? Do you have any enemies here?" One by one the people in my group were taken away until only an inmate named George remained with me.

Around 16 hours after processing began, George and I were ushered into Bellwood 1B1, our new home, a large barracks room about 50 x 70 feet in dimensions. The blare of the TV greeted my ear drums. Cigarette smoke assailed my throat as I made notes of the surroundings.

The paint is peeling off the walls which were painted a soft green in some bygone era. Double-decker bunks, about 60 beds in all, line three of the four walls and dominate the room visually. Ten nice, square tables occupy the center of the room, with four chairs attached to each table. The tables are for eating, TV viewing, games, writing, conversation, or whatever, including for me, witnessing for Christ.

This is Bellwood Barracks—Grand Central Station with no place to go. The bath area and officers' station are sandwiched in between 1B1 and 1B2, a second unit which also holds about 60 men. We share the same bath facilities, but are forbidden to enter the other unit. Officers stationed between the two barracks maintain round-the-clock surveillance of both units. This reduces the likelihood of serious physical harassment. These large units don't seem as threatening as the mental image I had formed of a typical jail. At night the lights are only dimmed, it's never dark here. I feel okay.

I got a grey, vinyl mattress and vinyl pillow to place on a metal upper or lower bunk. Along with this came two sheets, a pillow case, towel, and wash cloth.

One of my new barracks' mates looked at me. "Y'er due a toilet kit."

It took a couple of requests before I got the bare bones toilet starter kit. Beyond this, the inmate must purchase his own toothpaste, brush, deodorant, shampoo, et al. from the commissary.

I've settled in to what I expect will be my home for the next few weeks. Wearing the standard blue uniform, I don't stand out as I did when first brought into the jail. I'm going to pace myself in getting acquainted.

In the bath area I asked a wiry fellow with an unsmiling face what he thought of Jesus. He quickly replied, "I don't think much of Him anymore. Jesus used to be a possibility for me, but I'm a crook now."

"Jesus can still be the answer for you," I countered. But he was already retreating toward his bunk in 1B2 where I could not go.

Thursday, February 2.

Opportunities for witnessing have been falling into my lap. I was sitting on the lower bunk when an inmate with a toothy smile strolled over to get acquainted. "I'm Spud from Atlanta," he said. "Why are you here?"

I extended my hand and smiled back. "Glad to meet you, Spud. Sit down."

We hit it off easily. I found Spud to be one of those listeners who smiles when you're talking, as if to say "thank you" for every comment. He made me feel special just by sitting beside me and listening. He looked at my pictures of the mutilated unborn babies and grimaced. "That's terrible. It's enough to make ya sick. I'm against that."

After awhile I asked about his interest in spiritual things. "Which way would you go if you died tonight, Spud?"

"Well, I hope I've lived a good enough life to please God when my time comes."

I flipped to Romans 3:10 and passed the Bible to him. "Would you read that verse for me?"

He ran his finger down to the verse: "'As it is written, There is none righteous, no, not one.'" He looked up with puzzlement on his face.

"Spud, I can never please God with good works alone. If I could, wouldn't that make me my own saviour? Why would I need a Savior to come from heaven to save me?"

He blinked, but said nothing.

"Am I saved by my behavior or Jesus' blood?" I asked him.

"You're saved by Jesus, I reckon."

He listened closely as I took him through the plan of salvation. Then he knelt beside my bunk and invited Jesus to take control of his life."

Hallelujah!

My first full day in Bellwood Unit 1B1 has passed. The constant noise keeps breaking my thought patterns.

It isn't just the TV which has been blaring since I came in. With nothing else to do, the 55-60 inmates in 1B1 sit around smoking, playing dominoes, spades, checkers, chess; reading novels, arguing, cussing. Some appear to have no self control. A minor irritation in a card game, or a good play is reason enough for yelling, gleeful boasting, or cursing one's opposition. The swearing and outbursts seem to have become a form of recreation. Some give no indication of closing down at one a.m. I wonder when they sleep.

Friday, February 3.

Somebody must have turned the TV off—finally.

The din and smoke is a little better in the morning. It doesn't bother me as much. I'm looking forward to Mary's visit. I can see her already: a package of dark eyes, dark hair, warm smile. Gentle, selfless, giving. A petite four-foot ten sweetie with a giant heart for serving. At home I love to hear her lilting voice and laugh travel from room to room. Truly a Proverbs 31 wife. She's as happy working in the kitchen of a children's camp as serving on the board of a ladies Christian fellowship. *"Thank You, Lord, for my Mary. She's shown me what it means to be a servant."*

Ummm. I can smell her cooking. Southern corn bread just out of the oven, with just a touch of sugar. Ummm. I can taste her deserts. Once when I was trying to lose some weight, I suggested that she cut back on the deserts for me. She didn't want to do it. She felt a "need" to bake.

Breakfast comes early in this guest house. Visiting hours begin at 6:45 a.m. What if Mary has car trouble? An accident? *"Lord, watch over my dear Mary. Bring her to me safely."*

"Kerr, you have a visitor. The visitation booths are over in the main building. Come with me."

Step one in visitation is putting on the handcuffs. You then walk ahead of the officer in leaving the unit. The 150-yard walkway to the main building is fenced in and has closed circuit TV surveillance. There is a procedure for everything.

I walked gladly ahead of the officer and was escorted into the booth. Mary was on the other side, smiling at me through the glass, trim and cute in white pants and bold red and white striped sweater. I had the same blue outfit on that I wore yesterday.

"I left Mother and Daddy's at four this morning," she said through the phone, "and got here as soon as I could. The traffic wasn't all that bad. When I came into the jail, they checked my ID to see that I was on the visitors' list to see 'Inmate Kerr.' So, here I am." She told me later that she was struck by the loudness and coldness of the jail environment. She was instructed how to twist and turn through the cavernous building to finally arrive in the visitation area. It reminded her of a dungeon. "But if I can see my husband, it's all worth it," she decided.

The glass and phones through which we had to communicate seemed to dissolve. After years of marriage, we can read each other nonverbally and quickly. Her face told me she's making out okay. Her little brow wasn't wrinkled as I've seen it when she's worried. She's still with me all the way. We both sensed that we were adding

a dimension to our relationship, something rich and meaningful
that the world could not take away.
I shared with her my soul winning experiences. She rejoiced. And
as I had requested on the phone, she brought some cotton for my
ears to block out the TV noise at bed time.

Chapter 3

"The Church in Bellwood"

Friday, February 3, continued.

The cigarette smoke irritated my throat and made me cough. I walked over and stood under the fresh air ceiling fan which seemed to be the only place where there was clean air.

Idea! Maybe I can trade my bunk for the one right under the fan.

I approached a young black man whom I had met earlier. "Hey, Jerry, I'd like to offer you a deal. The smoke bothers me. I'd like to sleep by the fan. If you'd like to swap, I'll get some items on my commissary order for you."

He didn't say anything then, but did agree to the swap some time later. When my commissary order came [paid from the money I had left with a clerk], I gave Jerry the big arm load of candy and chips he had requested. Cost me $4.50, but it was worth it. Jerry was delighted and I got the location I needed for my cough. *"Thank you, Jesus!"*

When I moved my mattress, I got a surprise. My closest neighbor, who said his name was Harry, warned, "We're evil. You don't want to move over here."

I smiled at him. "I love Jesus, and can get along with anybody."

He didn't respond.

After being in this spot awhile I can agree with Harry's assessment of the wickedness around here. Unfortunately, the epidemic of vulgar talk is not limited to this new neighborhood.

Rather than shake the dust from my feet, I may just need to stay where the Lord has put me. Sin often needs to have its bluff called. Until a man realizes his lost state, how could he cry out to be delivered from it. Only drowning people cry out for help. I need to love him enough to encourage him to act on what the Spirit of God is already prompting him to do.

Harry came back and talked a little. He didn't show any spiritual openness, though I did ask him some soul-searching questions which I trust will in time seep through the concrete of his heart.

Later he moved his bed elsewhere. He just didn't want a minister around making him uncomfortable, I guess. That shows his conscience isn't dead yet.

Sunday, February 5.

Mark is a new acquaintance, of medium build, with glasses and a beard. Looks to be in his mid-thirties and has a low voice and easy-going manner. Regardless of what he's doing, when I visit his bunk, he's always friendly and glad I came. Says he is from Atlanta and owns his own T-shirt printing business.

He sits at a table and works on his business papers and accounts, just as he did at his office. He says he has a receipt in storage which proves he didn't steal the item for which he is in jail, but his problem is obtaining the receipt.

He professes to be a believer. I asked him, "Mark, what do you think of us starting a Bible study?"

"Yeah, it's OK by me."

Two other guys joined Mark and me on my bunk.

"Let's start with a hymn, fellows. How about 'Amazing Grace?'"

They knew the tune and some of the words. While we were singing, the other 50 or so guys in our 1B1 section of Bellwood went on watching TV, playing cards, yakking, cursing, reading, taking showers, going to the toilet, staring into space, or trying to sleep. Now and then one looked at us curiously. Nobody made fun.

I turned to the Gospel of John. It seemed best to give a simple overview of the book, then start back in the first chapter. They picked up quickly on the informal, question-answer format, as we read aloud verse by verse.

Before we knew it over an hour had passed. Willie, one of the fellows in the group, said, "Let's meet again tonight."

"Group, what do you think? It's up to you."

"Yeah." "Sure." "Good idea."

Eight came to the evening study. I had hoped Harry would be one of them, but he wasn't. The discussion flowed even better. They liked being drawn into a Bible passage, then asking questions.

"Was today just a fluke, Lord? Did eight come just because it was Sunday? Will they come again?"

Monday, February 6.

A letter from Mary!

Dearest Fred:

"God is our refuge and strength—a very present help in trouble." This has almost literally been felt, along with the prayers of my family. I got up this morning with a song on my lips and began praying not only for salvation of people in your barracks, but for miracles and healings to take place as well. This is just the type of thing that might help bring about the needed revival.

I hope you won't mind my staying here [with my parents] for a few more days. I like the comfort of Mom and Dad and since they are closer [to you than our home in West Columbia] I can get back quicker from visiting you.

Lots of prayer is going on [for you]. Nancy D., Linda B., Jan S., Glenn, and Sharon S. have called.

I'll stir up the body wherever I am—praise the Lord for what He is already doing . . . . God is faithful and good.

I love you with all my heart.

Mary.

My Mary is a woman of prayer. Her spiritual command center is in the guest bedroom at home. That's her place. The enemy has surely suffered some black eyes there.

Mary's prayer chamber is occupied mostly by my late grandmother's four poster bed and large, dark chifforobe. The bed is normally overlaid with an early American spread, three Bibles, at least one volume of **Matthew Henry's Commentary**, prayer notebook, hymn book, two devotional books, calendar, newspaper clippings, and other stuff that only she understands.

I've always sensed something special about that room. Once when showing it to Chinese students who had come for supper, I introduced it as, "this is where Mary prays."

Tuesday, February 7.

Wally is a new member of my "congregation." He admitted to me that he was addicted to the drug of nicotine. He has tried to break free many times, but confesses to have failed every time. "Ain't nuthin' that kin help me," he mourned.

I took him through the plan of salvation. He prayed to receive Jesus. I gave him a drug deliverance prayer: "Wally, tell Jesus what you want to do about your smoking. Ask the Lord to kick the Devil out of your life through His blood and power."

Wally prayed after me: "Lord, you know how many times I've tried to break the habit. Lord, take care of the old Devil. Get him off my back. You've got the power to do it. I believe you can. In Jesus' name, amen."

Are jail house decisions real? I suspect that an inmate of some days or even weeks tends to make a more solid decision than one arrested scant hours before. Still, it is just as easy to accept by faith that God is bringing prepared souls across your path as unprepared ones. Why not assume that the Holy Spirit has been at work in someone's life for many months or more likely, years?

Could it even be my ego assuming that one has not heard, really heard, the Gospel message unless I have personally presented it to him? I prefer to give the Spirit of God and the sinner the benefit of any doubt.

Once here, they at least have a respite from many worldly snares, where flesh can out shout the Spirit. While in this jail they may finally listen to the soft wind of eternity's whispers.

Why shouldn't a sizeable portion of fox hole and jail house decisions be as real as Jonah's repentance was inside the great fish? Was it not God who put Jonah in his underwater prison? Did that not result in Jonah finally responding to God?

Perhaps jail cells are the unsaved man's prayer closet. He finally has the time and place to get away from much of the worldly ear banging. At last he can sit, ponder, and decide where his life is headed.

Friday, February 10.

I was being escorted over to the main building again for visitation when the officer volunteered, "I'm interested in your philosophy. I'd like to talk further with you when I'm working your barracks again."

Hallelujah! Perhaps some officers here will follow in the footsteps of the Philippian jailer by crying out, "Sirs, what must I do to be saved?"

Sunday, February 12.

I still get my Christian magazines, now forwarded by Mary. Three can be sent in at a time. My time to read them is limited because I'm so busy with the ministry.

The first officer to show interest has not as yet sought me out. Another officer and a new friend asked if he could borrow one of the Christian magazines. He commented on returning it, "You don't know what this meant to me." It evidently helped to solve some big issue he was grappling with.

I asked him if he was saved. He indicated that he was. We discussed the things of the Lord. He maintained his professionalism, yet was friendly and conversive.

I've been leading Bible studies for a week now. The first one comes around 7:30 a.m, after morning head count, then we meet again about 7:30 p.m.

Excitement is mounting. The fellows now count participants as they see their Bible study continue to grow. They must sense that the Lord is in this study. Who doesn't want to be part of a meaningful new adventure?

It's doubly exciting to teach when you sense that some are experiencing their very first, real Bible study. We're still going through John, chapter by chapter. I'm teaching them to get the answers to my questions directly from the verse at hand. I try not to let them get by with barber shop opinionating about what "Aunt Susy" once thought a verse meant. I ask, "What does this verse tell us about why Jesus came to earth?" "What verse did you get that information from?" "What can we find out about Nicodemus just from verse one?"

I like the balance and thoroughness which the expositional, verse by verse, chapter by chapter method provides. I gear it down, telling many stories. Jesus told stories and parables. Stories bypass the literacy barrier some have. I just serve plain vanilla.

I told the men, "Think of this as a special Bible school which God has provided you. Remember that John the Baptist, the Apostle Paul, and Moses became men of spiritual power in the wilderness. Don't waste this precious time we have here together. Determine to leave different from the man who walked in. Read a book of the Bible every day while you're here. Time is no problem. Memorize verses. Develop your prayer life . . . ."

In our Bible study, some one said, "We need a name for this." In Bible study someone suggested we become a church. Another commented, "I've got it! The Church of Bellwood!" That pleased the "members" and it stuck. Bellwood church is a sanctuary for these men who have called upon the Lord for salvation. This may not

quite be a church as we think of one on the outside. We have a
variety of literature. But this church offers Bible study, worship,
prayer, fellowship, and encouragement of believers. In one way this
is even better than an "outside" church. Here the members are
denied access to sin for a season. That doesn't happen too often to
an outside congregation, unless the members go on a long retreat.

T.J. was one of those who received the Lord today. He has an
alcohol addiction.

T.J. took his alcohol problem to the Lord. He prayed after me,
"Lord, I am Yours. I want nothing that Satan has to offer. I am
cleansed by the blood of Jesus Christ, my Lord. I claim Christ's
blood for freedom. I claim Jesus' authority over my life.'"

I urged T.J. to repeat this spiritual victory prayer two, five, or
twenty times a day as needed, until the enemy is convinced his
former control is gone. I showed him James 4:7: "Submit yourselves
therefore to God. Resist the devil, and he will flee from you."

Chapter 4

"God Can Do Anything"

Monday, February 13.

A lean, lanky, long-haired, easy-going country boy named Steve joined us in 1B1 today. He's from L.A.—that's for "Lower Alabama," he says.

Steve is a carpenter by trade. He has a church background but got away from it. He still has a bullet in his jaw from the past.

I took him through the plan of salvation. Then we knelt on the gray blanket on my bunk, as others have done, and prayed for Jesus to wash all his sins away and sit on the throne of his life. As we finished praying, I asked, "Steve, where is Jesus now?" He replied in his slow drawl, "Wa'l, let's see. He must be around here somewhere?"

Richard is another character. Next to the TV, he is the single biggest contributor to the high noise level around here. Richard doesn't get many complaints. He's six foot three, with arms like stove pipes and looks as if he could handle two or three guys in a fight. He is allegedly on his way to a three-year term in the state prison on a drug charge.

Thankfully, Richard sleeps a lot. He makes up for his quiet snoring when awake. He's like a bear or lion that comes out of his den periodically to roar and reassert his authority. He shouts when things aren't going his way. He shouts for no apparent reason. He seems to shout for the sheer enjoyment of hearing his own roar. And, perhaps to relieve tension.

Even the domino games with his buddy, George Y., are punctuated with loud cursing and abusive arguments. I've decided that if God can save Richard, He can reach anybody here. We seem to have absolutely nothing in common, but then I don't know because I haven't been able to engage him in conversation.

Teaching the Bible over the blare of the TV is tough. The plaster walls and tiled floor don't absorb the noise. When Richard roars, I might as well shut up.

Wonder of wonders, Richard the shouter came to this morning's Bible study. He prayed to receive the Lord! I have to pinch myself to believe it. *"Thank You, Jesus. My ears as well as my heart both thank You."*
Four others also prayed to be saved today! The Lord is really moving!

I've tried not to make it easy or automatic to pray the sinner's prayer. I spend 20 to 40 minutes with each one before offering to pray. I only wish to know, "Do you really want to give it up?" I seek to deal with the particular sin which has the big hold on each fellow. If one isn't willing to confront particular sins before the cross, is he ready to be saved by the cross? One who isn't willing to give up fornication or drunkenness isn't willing to repent.
One big daddy sin—such as an immoral relationship or addiction to alcohol or another drug—can lower resistance to other sins. It holds the door open for more evil to enter. We don't inventory a man's sins. I'm only saying that there well may be one root sin, a pet sin, that must be addressed. Satan is using it to keep him from being saved. It must go.

Ted still looks like the massive, muscular football player he used to be. He was a big star in college who joined the pros lacking only a course or two to graduate. His whole life revolved around pro football, then the bottom fell out when he was cut from his pro team. He turned to alcohol and became more depressed. Now only in his late 20's, he can see no purpose or meaning in life.
He poured out his heart. "Only Jesus can give direction and electricity to your life," I told him. "That's how He wired us together."
We prayed. I asked, "Have you accepted Jesus into your heart?" He said, "Yes," but I can't see that the lights have switched on in him. Ted is still a "poor me, woe is me" type. I can relate to that. I used to be right where he is, attitude wise. *"Get him, Lord."*
Ted hasn't really plugged into the Bible study. I shared my heart with him. "Ted, discouragement is such a powerful tool of the devil. Don't let Satan keep his foot on your neck. The Bible study is your source of spiritual help, power, and food. You can't get strong

unless you eat. Can't you see what the enemy is doing? You need the discipline the Bible study brings. Don't dwell on yourself. Focus on God's wonderful promises."

Ted listened and nodded. But he still hasn't plugged in.

Tuesday, February 14.

Some of the personal counseling situations here are like counting a barrel of snakes. Sins are like bananas. They come in bunches. Only Jesus can fix them. He truly can.

I don't comment judgmentally when counseling these men, but seeing so much sin and hearing so much foul language hour after hour, all but a dead heart should become saddened. It's grieving to watch. There but for the grace of God go I.

The older I get the more I am convinced that one is saved totally by God's mercy. It's all of Jesus. It's all His reaching out to me in my ungodly and undeserving condition. It's 100 percent Jesus' dying and zero percent my doing. Like a man drowning in the lake, all one can do is yell, "Help!" Jesus hears and paddles the boat out to pull in the repentant sinner.

Many more are drowning too, but will not turn from sin and call out to Jesus. As Arthur Burt says, "If we're saved by grace, then good works won't bring it and bad works won't take it away."

Being here makes me thankful that God in His sovereignty chose to place me where I was somehow delivered from the drugs and dregs that have ravaged many here. Sin is so mean.

The outpouring of mail and support is uplifting and strengthening. It boosts my spirits to know that so many people around the country are interested in what God is doing in Bellwood Church.

Letters arrive from so many different states daily. They include offers of help and other encouragement, testimonies of similar experiences, Bible verses, stamps, money, return envelopes, prayer cards, poems, insights, and powerful thoughts. "But my God shall supply all your need according to His riches in glory by Christ Jesus" (Philippians 4:19). That was written by the Apostle Paul in jail!

Here's one from a fellow rescuer, a lady from Massachusetts:

```
Dear Fred:

    . . . The only time that I've ever spent in
jail was this past New Year's weekend when 40
of us . . . decided to stay until Tuesday. We
were seven to a tiny cell, there was no
```

ventilation, the heat was turned up to at least
90 degrees F., and they wouldn't let us have
much water. Actually it was a beautiful experience.

. . . Please know that there are great numbers
of people all around the country who support you
and are praying for you.

Praise God! The babies are not forgotten. And God has not
forgotten those who love these innocent babies who are seen by
many people as mere insignificant tissue.

Wednesday, February 15.

Praise the Lord! Richard the shouter has become Richard the
sheep. This quiet lamb has really plugged into our Bible study. His
disposition has totally changed. He's quiet. He mostly listens as
new believers usually do. I can't recall a single shout since he
prayed to receive Jesus. What God has done for Richard makes it
all worthwhile.

Others see the change in precious Richard. God has power
indeed. *"Lord, You are amazing. God, You can do anything!"*

Being here, one is able to discern changes in behavior more in
depth than at the "normal" church on Sunday. There a person can
smile and pretend for an hour or so. Here you can observe (and be
observed) round the clock, day after day. It's tough to hide very
long.

Sadly, Richard got shipped out one day after getting saved. He
cut it close. I know that's why God delayed his transfer from here.
I heard he went to state prison. We're praying for him.

Thursday, February 16.

B.T. and Max prayed to receive the Lord today. Max is rather
quiet and polite and doesn't offer much about himself. I haven't
had much opportunity to talk with him besides sharing Jesus.

Our little flock keeps growing. *"Thank You, Lord. You are so
faithful. How wonderful to be about Your work."*

The food here is better than I had expected. Much more than
"bread and water." Much better than the bologna sandwiches after
our arrest. Certainly there is some complaining, but the meals
could be much worse.

The apple cobbler is good. I also like the white beans fixed with
pepper. Some cooks really put the pepper on, others show mercy.

Our meals are brought over from the main building on carts by trustees with an officer. From kitchen to our tables can take 30-60 minutes, but it stays pretty warm.

Lots of swapping and bargaining occurs at meal times: "Two roll-ups for apple pie," someone shouts. "Roll ups" are roll-your-own cigarettes. A "Cadillac" is a cigarette from a store-bought pack.

Friday, February 17.

George Y., a middle-aged family man, came to Bible study this morning. He is formerly loud Richard's old domino partner. Wonder of wonders, George prayed to receive the Lord today. Wow! Did Richard's commitment influence his buddy for the Lord?

George Y. has been quieter. With Richard saved and gone and George Y. "saved," the noise level has come down considerably. Now if we could only get the TV saved.

I brought a book in with me by one of my heroes, revivalist and evangelist, Vance Havner. I've been reading some of his lines: "... Immorality is here to stay, but that is no alibi for making it respectable. ... Television is here to stay but we need not let it flood our homes with filth, because we are too lazy to supervise what we see or let others see."

We've got another new face. Greg is a little guy with short hair who talked tough until he came to Bible study and prayed the sinner's prayer. I also ministered deliverance to him.

Greg expects to be transferred in a day or two. With the constant turnover in this 60-bunk barracks, it's difficult to really get to know very many fellows well. It's like ministering on an escalator. *"Thank You, Lord, for keeping me in the same place."*

Saturday, February 18.

We had a triple header today. Terry, Bob, and Mac all prayed to receive the Lord. The angels in heaven must be having a jubilee. Glory! The Holy Spirit is on 24-hour call. It's simply amazing. I give God the glory for all these souls saved. I know no human could do it. For one who is no stranger to jail ministry in recent years (I've met prisoners and preached through the bars on Sunday morning back home), I know that the prayers of the saints are making the difference. Praise God for them. The battle is won in the prayer closet. God truly moves in response to prayer.

Each of these precious trophies of God's grace is different. Mac, for example, is a lanky, laid back guy with short hair. He listens more than he talks. It's hard to tell what he is thinking. He likes to take his food tray to his bunk and eat there. He isn't cocky or surly at all. He leaves other people alone, not being one to promote foolishness or disputes. His responses seem to be measured, not hasty. I hope he will follow through and make a serious commitment to the group rather than be rocky soil.

By God's grace, I use and encourage the brothers to employ four kinds of evangelism here: Friendship evangelism, marketplace evangelism, literature evangelism, and our Bible study with its altar calls. At times we have testimonies in the Bible study which confirm just how these methods do complement each other. Some are introduced to the Lord through friendship. Some pick up tracts or one of the Christian magazines which we leave in the bath area and eventually they come to the group meeting. Others respond better to the direct, bold approach which Jesus used with Nicodemus and the Pharisees. There's so much evangelistic freedom and power when we approach a person with truth and an earnest, caring attitude. Scriptural principles aren't at war with each other.

An evangelist is like an examining physician with a good bedside manner. He can say whatever he needs to say to the patient about a severe problem. He has the hurting person's respect whether the patient knows the doctor or not. He has a working relationship with the "patient" whether he knows him or not. God's love and God's truth aren't enemies but friends.

Such a physician must be bold. When speaking in churches on witnessing in the marketplace, I've repeatedly asked the congregation for a show of hands on this question: "Are most Christians too bold when witnessing or do most need more boldness?" The audiences have all agreed that most Christians need more boldness. I then confirm that "tonight, I'll be speaking to the majority of us who need more boldness."

Our Bible studies keep growing. My bed is at one end of the barracks. The TV is close to the other end. We meet on my bed and the believer's bed beside it. Here we are the maximum distance from the TV. Even though the volume is lowered when meeting, it's still quite intrusive.

We can sit four on each bunk. And the Lord has worked it out that the fellows living in the upstairs bunks attend also. That gives balcony seating, plus we scoot a table or two with attached chairs up to the bunks which provides seats for still more.

This setup seems preferable to meeting in the center of the room where the other table/chair units are. There, the TV is closer and louder and getting three or four of the tables with four-chair units close enough for all to hear is far from ideal.

God provides just what we need. He can do anything.

Chapter 5

"Am I Finished Now, Lord?"

Sunday, February 19.

I can leave! Our wonderful attorneys are appealing our cases to the Georgia State Appeals Court. Brenda and I can get out on an appeal bond of $1320 and $1760 any time we choose, if the money is available.

What do I do? I've been here almost three weeks.

Every Bible passage I've turned to has convicted me not to leave, even though I told Michael Hirsh [one of the leaders in Operation Rescue] that I was coming out.

Even a sermon on the radio convicted me that I should stay. I just don't have peace about leaving. I do have peace about being here at this time.

It's so important to be in tune with the Spirit of God in a situation like this. He can protect us from things we can't see. But the flesh nags to get its way. How relieving it is now that I've stopped wrestling with the Lord. He wants me here for now. I don't understand it, but it's OK. I feel at peace now that I've made this decision today. It's like resting after a grueling race.

Monday, February 20.

I talked with Matt Coles, one of our attorneys, on the phone. Mine and Brenda's appeal was entered today in the Appeals Court, but it will take at least two to five months to be heard. Attorneys Devin Ehrlich, Matt Coles, and I all thought that our sentences should be challenged—especially because 1,200 other rescuers, arrested in Atlanta this past summer and fall, are still awaiting trial.

Brenda is a godly woman with a zeal for God. She's been in a cell block which includes some hardened and immoral women. But fruit is coming out of it.

She even had a mild heart attack while here, leaving her husband very concerned. She has now decided to leave on the appeal bond. I had initially said I would depart also, but that was before God entered the ring with me. I'm now 0 for 3 with Him since our July 29 wrestling match of last year. I have no peace about leaving now, so I won't.

Brenda was released around supper time today. A reporter was waiting. Mary, who was in town to visit me, was there also. It must have been hard for my sweetie, knowing that I would not be coming out with Brenda.

Our Bible studies continue to go well. Bob, a new member of our flock, wanted to teach for the group. Mark, my co-leader, and I thought it would be OK. We need to raise up some leaders to take over when we get out. Bob did an amazingly good job for a young believer. I told him, "You'll be a really good teacher if you hang in there with Jesus and work at it."

Tuesday, February 21.

About one a.m. B.T. sought me out to talk. Said he's a pimp. He sees drugs as a dead end street, but expressed no longing to change. How typical of the Devil's strategy. He attacks the will, not just the mind. B.T. pointed to drug tracks on his arm. "This one," he said, "is a Rolls Royce, that one is a house, and that one is a boat. I'm also a hustler."

I told him plainly that "Satan is literally trying to kill you and Jesus is your only way out." He liked to talk, but didn't really seem interested in Jesus.

From talking with hundreds of people about salvation over the years I would put the unsaved in one of three groups: (1) Those under conviction of sin—"anxious" sinners, as one renowned revivalist called them. (2) Those open to listening to the plan of salvation. (3) Those not willing to listen to a simple explanation of how to be saved.

Those in category three include the disputers who resist earnest, direct talk about their soul's destiny. I use one or more of the following approaches with them:

Very early I try to ascertain their degree of interest with some watershed questions: "Do you know how to be saved?" Most will honestly admit that they do not. "Would you like me to explain the plan of salvation to you?" If they say no, I will likely not invest much effort on them at that time, but leave them with an earnest plea. I would beg if it would help: "Oh, friend, Jesus loves you. Don't run from Him. He wants to wash away your sins today. Let Him save you today."

I will not argue religion. "Answer not a fool according to his folly, lest you also be like unto him" (Proverbs 26:4). To an inmate who was into debating, I said, "I'm not here to argue, I'm here to talk to you about your soul. Would that interest you?"

I prefer to offer the defiant fellow one or more thought-provoking verses in love. I want to help him see and admit any defiant attitudes towards the Gospel. His precious soul is worth it.

Rambling, barber-shop discussions are usually useless. The natural man, the unsaved man, is skilled in dodging saving truth, or he might not still be lost. The effective soul winner is a professional with a specific assignment from the Lord. He's a spiritual obstetrician, not a talk show host.

Above all I want to be prayerfully listening and expecting the Holy Spirit to give me fresh thoughts and words which I may not have used before. The Holy Spirit is much more creative than I am, yet never violates the powerful, witnessing principles of the Word of God.

Wednesday, February 22.

I hear that Martin Luther King was housed in this same jail for leading a civil rights demonstration. I'm for the civil rights of the '60's —integration, and the civil rights of the '80's —the right to life. To ignore either is selective morality. The right to live is the most basic civil right. Without life all other rights are denied as well.

The Fulton County Jail has now been my home since January 31. I hear that 2100 men and women are in all the units of this jail. An officer said it was built for 900.

Twenty-three inmates have prayed to receive Jesus in the three weeks I've been in Bellwood 1B1. Two more prayed to be saved today. One prayed with Mark. Some decisions seem genuine, others questionable. It's always like that.

They need a lot of pastoral care. I repeatedly deal with sins of the tongue expressed by foul language, lying, silly talk, etc. I asked our group, "How much does the Devil pay to rent a fellow's mouth? Are any of us giving him free advertising?"

We're running nine to twelve in the daily Bible studies. A dozen new creatures in Christ singing "Power in the Blood" is surely putting some dents in the door of Hell. The supervising officers have made no complaints. God has truly given us favor. Our Bible studies, witnessing, singing, praying, and praising the Lord can only make their job of controlling behavior and attitudes easier.

I wonder how the jail administrators are reacting to the phenomenon in here. Surely word must have spread to them. Are they pleased? Will they move me to another location?

The men's commitment to our Bellwood fellowship is clear to all. We pray regularly as a group that our little church will be kept protected. It's all in the Lord's hands.

I want to give out a public statement on deciding to stay in jail for the present. With Brenda now out on appeal bond, some are likely wondering why I'm still here. I can only tell them that God must want me here. How do I explain something like that?

Mail call. Praise God! The officer reached through the opening between the chain link fence and the gate and handed me 18 letters. A big thank you to the concerned folks around the country who haven't forgotten me. Some of the letters come from caring pro-lifers. Some come from believers who have heard about me through the newspapers or some other source. They say, "Hang in there. We're praying. God will give you victory." I'm thankful for the encouragement. He is giving victory!

As I returned to my bunk with my daily treasure of mail, I had to take the customary walk past all the tables and chairs half filled with men watching TV, etc. Most rarely get any mail. Not one letter. Carrying my bundle of letters past their expressionless faces as they watched made me inwardly wince. I feel a bit sad for them yet I use the point to gently remind the church fellows, "Much of this mail is from Christians and pro-lifers elsewhere. They are helping me in many ways. This is what the Body of Christ is for. That's why you too need to be active in a church when you leave here. We need other believers. We need Christians to stand with us when we have needs. Their wonderful spiritual and financial assistance might be called a fringe benefit of commitment to the Body of Christ." I sensed that the point sunk home with them.

The most welcome letter came from my dear Mary:

My dearest husband,

The Lord is my strength and my song and He also has become my salvation.

. . . Your comments about the pastoral care really was a balm to my soul and spirit. There was so much that became clear and strengthened me for the next step. Thank you so much for sharing that.

. . . The work you are allowing Him to do [in you] gives me great courage and helps me to hold on to the Lord for myself as well.

This thing is from God. He will be our deliverer, and his deliverance will come at the appointed time. In the meantime, He will hold us fast.

I love you dearly,

Mary

Being here makes the memories of times spent with my Mary even more special. We love to walk our street with our German shepherd, Raisin, holding hands while talking over the events of the day, or praying together. Walking beneath the tall trees is a wonderful way to pray.

Thursday, February 23.

Twelve came for each of our two Bible studies today. We're still going through John chapter by chapter. We were in chapter 11 today, the story of Lazarus. I commented, "Fellows, here's how to remember which chapter Lazarus is in: E-L-E-V-E-N, Entwined Lazarus Emerged Victoriously, Entombed No (more)."

George Y., the domino king with the boisterous, profane tongue before his recent conversion, now faithfully attends. I've heard no bad or loud language from his lips since he asked Jesus to forgive his sins and to sanctify his mouth for holy speech. George is a wiry little guy. He's losing his hair like me. There is a seriousness about him. He says what he means, and doesn't speak lightly. He seems to mean business with Jesus.

"Lord, You can do anything! You have great power to work wonders."

Martin, a non-believer, had some candy and toilet items stolen from the drawer under his bunk today while he was in court. The officer investigating the theft began a shakedown. He put 57 or so men in the bathroom while their bunks and belongings were being searched. He exempted three of us in the Bible study because, "You fellows have proven yourselves."

"Thank you Jesus, for testifying through even such as we."

George Y., the domino player, offered Martin his own new toothbrush. Martin then agreed to drop his complaint. It was assumed the candy had already been eaten and wouldn't be located.

The officer halted the shakedown of the barracks. My heart was touched. God is working with George. Such a solution never occurred to me. I told him, "George, that was a fine thing you did."

Chapter 6

"Battling With the Basics"

Friday, February 24.

After the singing in this morning's Bible study I shared from a little pamphlet, "Help for Young Christians." It covers the ABC's of the believer's new walk with Jesus. The Christian life is won or lost in the battle of the basics, in the trenches of the fundamentals.

Because it's universally true that too many who make sincere decisions fail to go on with Jesus, I endlessly emphasize the basics of the Christian walk here in the unit. This continual spiritual kindergarten gets tiresome for the teacher at times, but I must not escape to more lofty teachings. Carpenters that tire of sawing and hammering aren't going to be very successful workmen.

I tell the fellows that after trying man's latest teachings and philosophies, we'll find God's deliverance and blessing where it has always been, in simple, old fashioned, Bible centered teaching. Some things don't change. Only our appreciation and discernment wavers.

"Forever, O Lord, Thy Word is settled in Heaven" (Psalm 119:89).

I asked our Bible study fellows, "Is it easier to walk 30 feet to church here or perhaps several miles out on the street? If a man can't make it to church in the unit how will he make it to church outside?" They got the point. Many need some industrial strength truth to fight the lions and tigers that will confront them in the drug and crime culture outside. I am plain and firm with them. Just giving a little pat on the back and a spoonful of spiritual whipped cream won't last.

"Iron sharpeneth iron; so a man sharpeneth the countenance of his friend" (Proverbs 27:17).

The mud-caked heart can't be hosed off with perfume, but needs the powerful Word of God.

We continue to average 10 to 12 in the Bible studies. Members keep getting released, so it's amazing how well the attendance holds up. God is surely in this. He is faithful.

Evangelism sometimes occurs in unusual places. During lingering moments in the bathroom today a fellow from the adjoining 1B2 unit and I began talking. After I shared Christ for a few minutes it became clear that he meant business about praying to receive the Lord. It was perhaps now or never as we were not supposed to socialize in the bath area. When I hesitated, he said "Well, are we gonna pray?" I sort of reluctantly led this stranger to the cross. What an interesting testimony he will have. What a rebuke for my reluctance. I should have known that God's hand is not so shortened that He cannot save—even in a jail bathroom.

After visitation today, I was escorted back from the main building by an officer who didn't handcuff me. That must mean he trusts me. I want to believe that Jesus' influence is spreading. Or perhaps at 150 pounds I just don't look fierce and powerful enough to escape.

It snowed yesterday. The low hit 20 with a 0 wind chill factor. That's C-O-L-D in Atlanta. It's cold in here today with the little heat that we get.

My heart is warm though. I just got some precious mail.

An 82-year old Indiana grandpa with 12 grandchildren wrote that he had been arrested for participating in a 1988 rescue. He prefaced his letter, "Praise and glory to our Lord Jesus Christ!" and signed it, "Yours, FOR LIFE."

Saturday, February 25.

In the morning Bible study we prayed about the need for heat. Now by six or seven p.m. it's hot. *"Thank You, Jesus for meeting real needs."* We had 11 for the p.m. Bible study. Two brothers had exchanged some hard words outside the group and Mark suggested we address this. I taught on John 13:34-35 and 1 Corinthians 13, the love chapter.

Operation Rescue was on the evening TV and radio news. Around 250 demonstrated and picketed. They asked Governor Joe Frank Harris to help on our cases. He spoke at the Atlanta pro-life rally recently on dealing with the unusual long sentences given to rescuers.

Missionary friend Tom Ashe stopped by to see me today. It took him over an hour to get in. The visit was good. Next week he will share our concerns for prayer with mutual friends.

A little while ago I noticed a big commotion over by the entrance to the unit. Inmates were crowding around a new trustee who was helping to deliver our linens. He's a well known soul singer, allegedly in jail for non-support of dependents.

Monday, February 27.

I got 51 letters today! Three days worth actually, but delivered to me on Monday. Mary wrote about Brenda Roberts' release last Monday.

> The Spirit, fire, and love flowed from Brenda as she came out. All the reporter got . . . was what God had done in there! It was beautiful. . . . Psalm 18 has been special to me today. In the early verses it speaks mostly of the righteous being rewarded through His righteousness that is placed on us. I am so glad you are standing up for this right. God's rewards are still to come.
>
> I love you—you are so precious.
>
> All my love, Mary.

That gal is a winner.

Mary also reported that our own state senator in South Carolina had called and offered to write letters to officials in Georgia for me. Another state legislator wrote me:

> I admire what you are doing and only hope that your early release is eminent . . . . I . . . assure you that you are not alone in these feelings [about the slaughter of the unborn] and maybe shortly, with God's help, we can put an end to both the suffering of the unborn and of people like yourself that are striving against this issue.

I also heard from several pastors. One said:

> I pray for your strength and endurance during this difficult ordeal. At the same time, and even more, I pray that you will be able to rejoice that you are counted worthy to suffer for Christ's sake. I pray that your suffering will

be with great joy and thereby of benefit to you
to witness to others.

I just did a washing with my hand soap bar, using the lavatory
bowl. I can't get my clothes fully clean, but they smell better.

I swapped my eggs, sausage, and bread this morning for two-
and-one-half pints of pure orange juice. I'm staying with my low
cholesterol diet rather well, so far.

Twelve came to the a.m. Bible study. I shared with the guys
Psalm 3: David's problem, verses 1, 2; David's Protector, 3, 4;
David's peace, 5, 6; David's power, 7, 8. Mark then continued
through a Bible study guide on the basics of the Christian life.
Several shared prayer needs, including upcoming court appearan-
ces, lawyer hassles, and family circumstances.

Last night in our study I asked, "How many will try to witness
to someone in the next 24 hours?" Most raised their hands and
there has been some sharing today.

Scott brought a new fellow, Andy, to the group this morning.
Scott and another brother had been going through the plan of
salvation booklet with him.

Yesterday, Mark, and I were not on the list of names read out to
attend the Chaplain's Sunday afternoon worship service. This is
the second time in four Sundays that this has occurred. I'm puzzled.

I've had no visitors since last Wednesday. That's unusual. I enjoy
having a visitor, though it can also take about one-and-a-half to
two hours for even a half hour visit. You wait 15-30 minutes after
getting notice from the sergeant. It takes another 15 minutes to
walk to the visitation booth in the main building. After the visit
you can wait up to 45 minutes for an officer to come and escort you
from the booth.

Officers interpret regulations differently as is done in the Army.
One may be busy with other duties which results in you getting
extra time with your wife.

They're suppose to search you after visitation to prevent drugs
and weapons from being slipped in. This is usually just a quick
frisk with feet spread apart and hands up the wall. A few ask you

to take off your shoes so they can bend them to check for blades. I'm glad for the drugs and weapons checks. Some search you well, others do not. It varies with how well they know you and whether they smell trouble or not. I imagine it helps to be a good judge of character in this profession.

I look forward to visitation for another not so obvious reason. Between the time my visitor leaves and the officer comes to get me, I can really be by myself. I pull out my list of favorite hymns and praise choruses and rejoice. The singing touches something deep within me. I need this regular battery recharging time. I'm strengthened. My spirits are lifted. I leave in a different frame of mind.

The booths are sort of private and unsuspecting pedestrians passing by can flee as desired. Many people operate one or two quarts low on praise anyway. It won't hurt them.

One officer walking by heard me singing and stopped to ask, "Who are you?"

"Fred Kerr," I replied. I presumed he was interested in spiritual things or he would not have inquired. Being in the midst of praise and worship, I felt I was only about three feet from Heaven's door anyway. I asked the officer, "Have you been born again?"

"Yes," he confirmed. We talked. He left saying, "Keep on praising the Lord."

We are to "declare His glory among the heathen, His wonders among all people. . . . Let the heavens rejoice, and let the earth be glad; let the sea roar, and the fullness thereof. Let the field be joyful, and all that is therein: then shall all the trees of the wood rejoice" (Psalm 96:3,11,12).

Some trustees and officers whom I've gotten to know now smile and wave when they see me coming and going to visitation in the main building. Others I can't recall meeting call me "Rev" and offer greetings. I'm usually handcuffed when walking the halls, so shaking hands isn't possible. It's a strict environment, but not without friendliness.

You can't actually see faith, but you can watch believers praising Him. Praise can be zeal for God with the wrapping removed. Praise is our faith standing up tall. It's serving appreciation to our wonderful Savior on a silver tray. Though no substitute for daily obedience, Scripture does not call us to choose between praise or faith. It is a powerful manifestation of faith. Robust praise can be our heart for God in full dress uniform. I really need to ask the Spirit of God for a daily filling every morning. I don't want to be one of those who limps and gasps his way to Heaven.

I had some extra time of quiet prayer yesterday while lying on my bunk. I need to do that more often. Prayer is hard work.

During my daily devotions I often walk around our barracks room reading in a low voice, singing or praying to myself. When I first began doing this, I wondered if I was violating Matthew 6:5, 6 which tells us not to pray to be seen by men as the Pharisees do. I've decided that this is just continuing what I was doing at home as I paced around the kitchen or my office and prayed. As I know my heart before the Lord, I'm not doing this to be seen of men. I would prefer to walk and pray totally alone in the morning, but cannot while here. Motive is the key.

My quiet prayer stroll about the barracks seems to enhance ministry opportunities also. New people will come to me to talk and share problems or ask for prayer. I can then minister Jesus' deliverance, love, and saving truth.

For a few, the prayer stroll may encourage their vile tongue. Darkness doesn't like to have its nature exposed. Yet they can't escape it. They're stuck in here with me. So they may be venting the discomfort in their spirit through about the only socially approved means here, filthy language. Most walked into this barracks already cussing, though.

Most of my fellow inmates call me, "Rev," "Reverend Kerr," or "Brother Fred." Even among the most unbelieving inmates there is at least a distant respect for ministers. That may even open a few doors.

One astute member of the Bible study pointed out that the Bible doesn't call anyone "Reverend." I agreed and commented, "That's why I prefer to be called 'Brother.' All born again people are to be ministers, some are pastors. All are brothers and sisters."

Tuesday, February 28.

There has been mild tension in the barracks for a couple of days because of a few unusual disagreements. Two of our Bible study members made unkind, unnecessary, and angry comments to others in and beyond the church. An early morning shoving match between two members also erupted. I drew them aside for counsel.

"What do you think Jesus would have done in that situation? Isaiah 30:15 says, 'In quietness and in confidence is your strength.' What kind of witness is this to the fellows not in our church?

"Proverbs speaks of arising quietly in the early morning. I like to begin with God, not man. I want to get up with thoughts on the Lord. . . . Do you think this [altercation] would have happened if we had all spent time with the Lord this morning? Bible reading and prayer gives us strength to resist temptation."

They sat quietly. The counsel was sinking in. "Are each of you willing to forgive the other?" I asked.

They nodded and shook hands, but one left happier than the other.

I see the tension as a counterattack on the Lord's work here. I decided to do the evening Bible study on a passage dealing with attitudes, love, and the tongue. I began: "Today, let's have a real prayer meeting as we pray through these verses in Colossians, chapters three and four. Pick any verse and pray about what it says." We prayed that God might overcome the spirit of anger and confusion that seemed to have invaded the barracks.

I feel like a camp counselor ministering to a bunch of mostly unsaved campers. This is a wonderful, short term missions opportunity.

I've never had so many openings to witness. Chess games, shaving, washing clothes, bunk talks, almost anything leads to an opportunity. Over the years, I've developed a two sentence testimony, a five-minute version, and a ten-minute version. Often the two-sentence witness will lead to a full presentation of the plan of salvation. When I speak of bold witnessing I am commenting largely in the context of witnessing to strangers and casual acquaintances that pass through our lives each week. I'm not primarily referring to reaching close friends and family. Many Christians would agree that more boldness across the board is needed though.

By meditating and staying full of the Word of God and the Spirit of God, I can have answers apt for any occasion. As Ruth Graham said, "minister out of the overflow." Or as the late evangelist Lester Roloff used to say: "Go to town with a full wagon, not one half empty."

Chapter 7

"Thoughts on Baby Killing"

Wednesday, March 1.

Michael Hirsh came to see me yesterday. We enjoyed good fellowship. Michael asked for permission to try and get me out on a signature bond. I am leaning toward "yes" but want to hear from God first. I believe He has yet more for me to do in the Bellwood barracks.

If I had my druthers, I'd be home with Mary tonight. But I keep thinking of the babies. If I can just keep one more little one from the suction and the knife, it will all be worthwhile.

God's Word has some very specific things to say about killing innocent children. In Leviticus 20:1-3, God instructed Moses to tell Israel and "the strangers that sojourn in Israel . . .Whosoever . . . giveth any of his seed unto Molech; he shall surely be put to death; the people of the land shall stone him with stones. And I will set my face against that man, and will cut him off from among his people because he hath given of his seed to Molech, to defile my sanctuary, and to profane my holy name."

This passage says:

(1) Molech is the god of child (and human) sacrifice.

(2) Killing one's children is evil for both God's children and others (sojourners) as well. Every one in the land was covered by God's command.

(3) They were not to ignore others who killed children. God's commands were for all the people, not just Moses or the leaders. The Israelites themselves were accountable to understand this important issue.

(4) God's sanctuary and His holy name are defiled by child sacrifice. Child sacrifice is a high priority issue with God. I have no doubt that the Biblical prophets would be on the firing line against legalized abortion if they were living in America today.

God pulls no punches in His Word. He is not pro-choice when it comes to murdering babies. He is not the Lord of some pluralistic religion, where those who profess His name can kill their babies, or even permit others to sacrifice their unborn ones in the arbortuary temple to the god of convenience. They can't be troubled with bringing up the little ones God has given them. And to think that some politicians and even so-called ministers praise them for exercising responsible freedom of choice. God help us!

I sense that many believers are truly grieved over the killing of 4,000 unborn babies every day. They would vote abortion on demand out in a minute if they could. Yet they think, as I once did, "How much good can I do? The Supreme Court alone has the authority to reverse Roe v. Wade."

Why has there been such silence from so many of the 300,000 American pulpits since Roe v. Wade in 1973? Why has most action come from small, under-financed pro-life groups and some Christian media? Even with the big push on family-related issues today, protecting the unborn has received scant lip service. Except for passing mention in sermons and token appearances at rallies, support is weak from the ordained ministry.

Thank God for James Dobson, Jerry Falwell, Tim and Beverly LaHaye, Phyllis Schlafly, Richard Land, James Kennedy, Pat Robertson, Randall Terry, Dr. John Wilke, and others who have not been silent about this monstrous evil. I pray God will raise up many more of their courageous kind. I'm impressed to pray for pastors' hearts and consciences to be concerned about baby killing. The average Protestant church member has had very little teaching on abortion since Roe v. Wade made abortion on demand legal. Many Bible-believing church leaders are pro-life technically and intellectually, but not practically. The sanctity of life has not been taught very much from Protestant pulpits. Many pastors have not been enthusiastic about bringing in films about this terrible infanticide. The typical, submissive church member will not go beyond the leadership of his pastor. They await the pastor's signal to join one of a number of pro-life groups.

Some pastors are aware of members who have had abortions. These pastors may have counseled and comforted them. Possibly they won't teach on the issue for fear of stirring up hurt or alienation in the congregation. Yet is this a greater hurt than what 4,000 babies experience each day?

Certainly there are ongoing consequences of an abortion. That's another reason why it is so wrong. God is trying to spare us the devastating after effects. So is the answer not to teach on it?

Forgiveness for sin, including baby killing, is available in Jesus Christ alone. We need to teach on it if only for this reason.

A brother in our church just told me about an incident that happened at 4:30 one morning. One of the inmates climbed the high chain link fence which separates our barracks from the officers' station. He was roughing up a female guard trying to prevent his escape. A second inmate who saw what was happening climbed the fence to help the guard.

The second inmate was surely violating a jail ordinance in climbing the fence. He put himself at risk. The escapee could have attacked him. Other officers coming on the scene could have thought he was escaping and injured him. Still he went ahead because he believed that human life was more important than no trespassing signs, property rights, and personal inconvenience.

When life is being threatened the caring person is not apathetic. He or she acts to try and save that life.

A common slogan today is, "Doesn't a woman have a right over her own body?" This is a misleading question. Two bodies are involved, not just hers. There are two heartbeats, two blood types, and half the time the sex of the baby is even different from her's. The question avoids responsibility.

A woman certainly has rights as well as responsibility over her body. And it starts before the sex acts begins. Not after some unwanted problem occurs. AIDS has powerfully reminded us of that.

And once exercising the right to have sex, the die has been cast. Choices have been made. If a person drives recklessly and hits someone he cannot leave the scene of the accident prematurely claiming his "right" to do so.

Suppose one wanders into a car dealership and on impulse, special orders a car. Then in two weeks the salesman calls saying, "The car you ordered is here." Then suppose the customer takes an ax down to the dealer's shouting, "I don't have to accept responsibility for this car. I have my rights." And proceeds to break the windows, headlights, and destroy that fine, new car. Is that acceptable behavior?

Neither can the woman who exercises her right to have sex and does so duck her moral responsibility.

Chapter 8

"Life Among the Brethren"

Friday, March 3.

I heard today that word has spread of the working of God here in Bellwood to Jackson State Prison in Milledgeville, Georgia, and revival has broken out there! *"Move in Milledgeville, Holy Spirit."*

Three more members of our Bellwood church got released yesterday, T.J., George Y., and Gregg.

The dramatic change in George Y.'s life was a testimony to us all. Overnight, after he took Jesus into his heart, he changed from a wild man to a gentle, attentive, faithful church member. He came so faithfully to worship and Bible study.

Bellwood Church has now had four released in three days. The releases from our fellowship are amazing when considered in ratio to the total number here. I'm secretly disappointed to see so many of our brethren go. I would like some of them to stay and feed on the Word longer.

Our prayers follow them. We exchange addresses so that we can stay in touch on the outside.

The many releases coming from our group is impacting other inmates who were previously uninterested in us. They want in on this "escape route" to freedom. They can give you the count of our church members released for the week. Will some now join our group and become only "rice Christians?" I try to discourage using God as an escort service to get out of jail. Jesus wants to be Lord, not a latch key. The angel freed God's man, Peter, from jail, not the rest of the prisoners in the Jerusalem jail. (Acts 12:6-9)

The teaching of God's Word, under the enabling of the Spirit, is the way to deal with this problem.

I've been teaching again on the difference between salvation by faith in Jesus and salvation by human works. Many are foggy on this.

I asked the brethren again today, "Am I saved by my doing or by Jesus' dying? Is it my service or His sacrifice? My grit or God's gift?

"Friends, if I add anything to the saving blood of Jesus, am I not spitting on the sacrifice of the Lamb? Am I not saying that His 'once for all' sacrifice was not really once for all, but insufficient, temporary, or ineffective? To think that my good works could in any measure help pay for my sins before a holy God is like offering John D. Rockefeller 50 cents for a cup of coffee. God doesn't want our tips, or a bit more of our time. He wants to give unsaved sinners the free gift of eternal life. We don't deserve it. We cannot earn it or it would no longer be a gift. There are only two kinds of people in the world, unforgiven sinners and forgiven sinners. I'm not saved because I'm good. I'm good because I'm saved.

"I'm not a perfect man, I'm a forgiven man. And, because I'm forgiven, God sees me as perfect in His sight. Can you say 'Amen' to that?"

They could.

"Now that I'm forgiven, does this mean that life is going to be 'easy street' from here on? No, the Lord promised, in John 16:33, that 'in the world you shall have tribulation: but be of good cheer; I have overcome the world.' If I'm obedient to my Saviour, life may be even tougher than it was before. Am I not in jail for protecting innocent life?"

They seemed to get the point.

Saturday, March 4.

No visitors today. I'm recovering from some bug. My throat and voice are still weak, the cough I've had for a good while persists. When I'm around a smoker my throat still complains loudly. I'm a jogger. I know smoke isn't good for lungs.

I've been a jogger or fast walker for 23 years. Here I jog slowly around the room for 20 minutes, then follow with two or three other exercises. The jogging felt good today, but the bug has delayed my full return to exercising.

Mark and I now have a training class for Bible study leaders. I use some of the same teaching methods which I found effective during my days as an InterVarsity Christian Fellowship campus staff member. We had three of these classes today with questions, answers, and assigned homework.

We'd have more brothers in this leadership class if so many hadn't been released. We hate to see them depart so soon, but our hearts follow them and we pray that they will develop their potential in some other fellowship.

Praise His name! We had the largest crowd yet at our Bible study tonight—14.

Two new men attended. One of them, Dan, is from my home state of Tennessee. He's a soft-spoken boy, raised as I was sort of back in the woods. He needs to step out into the spiritual sunshine.

Brother Mark and I are continuing through the book of John. Tonight we intended to study John 18, 19, but the opening songs and praise led us to focus on the second coming of the Lord. I continued on that line, sharing from Revelation 19, Matthew 24, 25, and I Thessalonians 4:16-18.

What a ministry opportunity I have here. It's all one could desire. I teach, witness and win souls, disciple one-to-one, direct memory work, lead songs, counsel, pray, praise, and enjoy good fellowship. As Sid McCollum, a former InterVarsity leader, would say, "Just pitch a little hay in every stall."

My days are busy though my time is 98 percent free time. There are no regular work details here. Still I can't get everything done in a day that I would like to do. Besides the ministry preparation and sharing opportunities, I also read the mail, write Mary and key correspondents, chat with friends, meet new people, visit with pastors and attorneys, etc., receive edification from radio teachers, make phone calls, read magazines, keep writing this journal, talk with officers, and get in some exercise, recreation, and occasional naps. In addition, I'm responsible for washing my clothes by hand, making the bed, and changing linens.

I often don't plop in bed until midnight or one a.m. The nights are short, as we are awakened for breakfast about 5:45. Amazingly I can now get by on much less sleep than my normal eight hours at home. Five to six hours is my norm here. God's grace is practical.

Again and again I silently delight at how well my co-leader, Mark and I flow together. We've yet to have a disagreement, though we come from totally different subcultures. We've got the blood of Jesus in common. "So then you are no longer strangers and aliens, but you are fellow citizens with the saints, and are of God's household. . . . in whom you also are being built together into a dwelling of God in the Spirit" (Ephesians 2:19,22, NASV).

Some of the brothers are here for seemingly trite, or even unfair reasons (according to what they say). Joe bought $250 of nice, used furniture from the security guard in the basement of his condo building. The pest control man recognized it and here Joe is. The furniture had been stolen.

Paul is a likeable, easy-going, fellow from Georgia. He was an orphan of sorts with the nicest smile. Before coming here, his business was buying and reselling trade-in tires from retailers. He hired a stranger with a truck to pick up and deliver a load of tires, but the fellow took them home instead. When Paul went to unload the truck himself, the fellow shot at him several times with a .357 magnum pistol at close range and missed!

"God's angels were watching over you!" I offered.

"They sure were," he excitedly confirmed, then noted that the other fellow was charged with unlawfully firing a firearm in the city limits, while he, Paul, was charged with stealing his own tires.

He tells that story over and over. Either it made a deep impression on him or he likes to tell a good tale. It's some of both I think.

Everybody has a story. Reinhold claims he has memorized 9,000 Bible verses. When asked to share some of them, he went dry after giving only one or two well known verses.

Billy Joe told me he had sold crack. "How could you do that knowing how dangerous it is to users?" I asked.

"When you're only making four or five bucks an hour," he replied, "a thousand dollars a day becomes tempting."

I spend a lot of time listening.

Fourteen of the 57 inmates in this room came to Bible study tonight. That's a fourth, lacking one man, of the Bellwood population! That's my one month anniversary present. Who would have thought it? *"Lord, I give You the glory and praise!"*

Sunday, March 5.

Twelve came to morning Bible study which Mark led from the Bible basics study guide he's teaching through. A caring Christian sent the new guide from South Carolina. Three new fellows, who had been here a few days, helped replace some of our releases. The new guys are in their late teens, playful, but worldly and foul-mouthed. Unsaved folks often act like unsaved folks. Sometimes saved people do too.

Bellwood got more new guests this morning. My first impression of Jerry when he arrived was not good. He looked sullen and defiant. Is he just trying to come on tough, or is he really a mean one? I wondered. I decided he wasn't the type I could relate to. He's too much like a street tough. My natural man whispered, "Maybe he's not the kind to respond to friendship or bold evangelism."

I had second thoughts while waiting in the lunch line near him. We got to talking. He came to the group and prayed to receive the Lord!

Jerry's about 23, tall, muscular, with a certain style in his walk. He's the kind you'd want on your side in a physical confrontation. The scrapper even beat me in a game of chess.

He's here for backsliding at a drug rehab center. Workers just laid out some stuff in front of him at his job and he couldn't resist. He really disappointed himself. After he serves his time here, he'll have to go back to the rehab center when an opening occurs.

I just finished a daily devotional with Jerry. I read Proverbs 15 to help him deal with some of the folly and foolishness being spouted by some of his unsaved friends in the barracks. "I'm glad you're here," he smiled. That really made me feel appreciated. "I'm glad you're here, too," I declared.

He thought I meant that I was glad he was here to protect me from harm. He said with confident cheerfulness,"I'm not going to let anything happen to you."

I didn't try to clear up his misunderstanding, but let his kind offer stand. I saw again how much influence one can have in young lives by reaching out in friendship. Jerry is a reminder not to assume one's self out of the harvesting business by prejudging who will respond and who won't. Sometimes the tall and the tough fall first. Now he's really special to me in the Lord, and he's got leadership potential. *"Jesus, keep Jerry from the Evil One."*

On the way back from visitation today I got to share my testimony with two other Bellwood residents also waiting for an escort back to our barracks. I told them, "I don't want anything to do with religion. Religion kills, but Jesus gives life. Religion is Satan's counterfeit. Hell will be filled with religious people. God, through our faith in Jesus, will make us righteous people. You fellows can do what I did. You can invite him into your heart today."

I've found that it helps to write out my testimony. This, along with sharing it verbally, helps keep my relationship with Jesus fresh.

I come from a long line of Baptist preachers on my mother's side and Methodist on my father's. I recall Grandmother Kerr telling us kids of our forbearer, Pastor Scarlet: "He was martyred while pastoring his church in the yellow fever epidemic in Memphis in the 1800's. You come from fine men."

Grandmother Kerr believed in straight living and was not bashful about sharing her views with family members, young and old. She knew how to impart high moral values. She would tell us grandkids about admirable qualities that our ancestors possessed. No doubt we had our share of horse thieves back up the line, too, but I never thought to ask about them.

She was as quick to give us youngsters a little money when visiting her as she was to deliver a straight, moral talk on how to live. She was raised in rural Tennessee. She didn't like doctors, dentists, medicine, or airplanes and lived mostly without them into her nineties.

At the Kirtley reunions when my mother's kin gets together, my "retired" Aunt Jean Molloy occasionally will bring out the treasured book with the story of great-grandfather James Kirtley. With a glint in her eye she recounts the character of this preacher in a rough-and-tumble Kentucky town.

The faded old book reveals the story. It seems that a traveling Jewish salesman, Felix Moses, had the misfortune to be passing through this town when a crude woodsman named Tim appeared. Upon learning the stranger was a Jew, Tim charged like a bull, intent on killing him. With Tim's rough hands not far from the Jew's throat, a second man intervened and the fight to decide Felix Moses' fate was ready to begin.

Just then Pastor James Kirtley arrived in his buggy. In his black preaching suit, hat, and neatly trimmed beard, my preacher ancestor was a commanding figure with a gentlemanly bearing. With a few words and some choice scriptures, he "turned enemies into friends." He helped Tim to see the error of his ways. Then he took the Jew home with him.

Felix Moses told Pastor Kirtley, "You haf saved mein life." Then he pulled out a large family diamond and gave it to great grandfather Kirtley. My forbear looked at the jewel and returned it to the salesman, saying quietly, "I do not need jewels. I hope always to be your friend and to claim you as one of mine. You may sometime need money, and this jewel should bring you a considerable sum."

I would like to think of Grandpa Kirtley and Pastor Scarlet as among the "cloud of witnesses" smiling down from Heaven at our church in Bellwood.

I was raised in a lukewarm church in Tennessee where you were probably assumed to be a Christian if you attended services. I can't remember ever being questioned about my salvation or eternal destiny.

I joined the church when I was twelve and was active through college. Then in my early 20's, while working in Knoxville, I dropped out of church totally. I was angry at God because He didn't seem to meet my needs.

Dating and tennis didn't fill the void. As soon as the fun or recreation was over, the loneliness returned. Then at 29 I met some new friends through tennis. They spoke of Jesus on Tuesday and Thursday, as well as on Sunday. They laughed a lot and had a peace that I didn't have. They were different.

They invited me to a home Bible study. That too was different for me. They had a purpose and direction in their lives. I checked them out for several months. I didn't see myself as a lost sinner—yet. I saw no urgency to repent.

Then one afternoon while lying on my bed and reading a Christian magazine, a verse from Romans jumped out at me. Something about God loving us and dying for us while we were yet sinners. Now I wasn't waiting on God to meet my needs. He was waiting on me! It was an eye opener. The ball was in my court. It was my move. I was the one holding out.

I looked up one of my Christian friends, and in a living room in West Knoxville about midnight on a Saturday evening, December 21, 1968, I asked forgiveness for my sins and invited Jesus to come and be the pilot of my life. I announced it to the home Bible study the next day. It was touching to learn they had been praying for me.

As a new babe in Christ, I didn't know much. I did know that I had turned a big corner. Something had happened and it was good. In the 21 years since, I've never doubted or regretted that decision.

We've been meeting twice daily, seven days a week, for over a month now. Yet only half of the 30, praying to receive Jesus, have plugged into our church group. The other half reminds me of the drunk who told the great preacher D.L. Moody that he was one of his converts. Moody replied, "You must be, you're certainly not one of the Lord's." An earlier evangelist, George Whitefield was asked how many had been converted in his meeting that day. Whitefield said it would take a month or two to find out.

At 11:30 this morning I saw sleepy-headed Paul getting out of bed. Paul stays up until all hours and then can't rise for the 7:30 a.m. Bible study of regular spiritual feeding. I admonished him about discipline and daily priorities: "The Bible and prayer is the way the Spirit 'pumps iron' to add muscle strength. Without these divine aids your spirit won't be strong enough to resist compromising. When you get out, you won't make it on the street without walking close to Jesus. I care about you, Brother. Do you believe that?"

Paul blinked his eyes. "Yeah."

I must keep nudging the brothers to use their time wisely and give priority to spiritual food while they're in Bellwood. With such high turnover, I'll have to settle for getting them saved and putting a few foundational principles under their belts. In Acts 8, Philip could only introduce the Ethiopian eunuch to Jesus and baptize him. Personal discipleship was not the will of the Spirit (vs. 38).

Many of our brothers need much more than normal discipling and follow up. They should have a six to twelve month discipleship program.

The drug addicts and some others know how to be manipulative and rebellious toward authority. They lack the most basic discipline. Some complain at even having to get out of bed for head count. They are still children in adult bodies.

Such personality patterns and emotional underdevelopment won't be changed overnight. A godly boot camp could provide the father figures and role models some have been robbed of while growing up. I can only hope to provide a little of that here.

In the evening Bible study I taught on the trial and crucifixion of Jesus. Here are some of the Bible's saddest verses. One of the 12 who had been with Jesus for up to three years and seen countless signs and wonders, betrayed Jesus.

The soldiers whipped Jesus, pushed a crown of thorns into his tender scalp, and shouted, "Hail, King of the Jews!" Pilate presented him to the chief priests, declaring, "Behold the man!"

The chief priests screamed back,"Crucify Him, crucify Him" (John 19:1-6).

I told the brothers, "In Christ's time, high religious offices didn't always testify of the new birth or even truthfulness. So it is today. When hard times come, we too must look beyond the modern, cotton candy crosses and record album religion."

After tonight's Bible study, I ministered for almost three solid hours to Dan, the new boy from Tennessee. Dan prayed to give his heart to the Lord. It's bedtime. Time for Dan and me to get some sleep.

Chapter 9

"The Spirit Keeps Moving"

Monday, March 6.

My cholesterol was 251 just before coming in here. The doctor had me on a low cholesterol diet. He sent a letter to the jail medic who told me, "We're not set up for special diets. We do well to deal with the diabetics. But I can give you a chart for evaluating cholesterol content in food items though." The chart has been most helpful. *"Thank You, Lord."*

Grits are a constant on the Bellwood breakfast tray, along with scrambled eggs, bread, a meat patty or weiner, milk, and coffee. We get orange juice only two or three mornings a week.

Grits is "southern snow." Mixed with a bit of pepper, salt, and margarine, it's okay. On Saturdays we get dry box cereal for variety. This is a treat we look forward to.

There's a lot of swapping around. This morning I made a touchdown. By trading the high cholesterol items, plus paybacks from prior trades, I got six half-pints of pure orange juice! God is so good. *"Thank You, Jesus."*

I called Mary last week. She followed up with a letter that arrived this morning. "Dearest husband," she began, as she did in the previous letter. I love that. She rejoices with me over what the Lord is doing here. She's not a complainer.

I miss my bride of 16 summers. I relive precious memories. I proposed to Mary in the Smoky Mountains at Cades Cove. Before the nearly two hour drive up there, I said to the Lord, "If it is not your will for us to get married, let us have a flat tire on the way." Then I thought anybody could have a flat tire, so I changed my request to, "Lord, let us have two flat tires. That will be the sign not to get married." We had no flats and by His grace our marriage has kept on rolling, too. God hasn't given us any children, although we love to spend time with our nephews and nieces.

The Smokies also bring back other memories. Living nearby for years, I've spent some time in the coolness of those deep, green mountains. I have a special place that calls me back to visit. A crystal clear stream cascades over and around smooth rocks. Then it gathers in quiet pools to rest awhile. There's a slow motion peacefulness about this stream, over which the lush, timeless mountains rise like majestic road signs pointing toward God Himself.

Tuesday, March 7.

Leonard, who has hitherto been unresponsive to my spiritual prods, came and asked to talk. He admitted the need to turn his life around. He prayed to receive Jesus a half hour later.

The smoke bothered my throat so much I was gasping out the prayer. The cigarette smoke is my toughest physical challenge, with the hellevision, blaring 16-18 hours a day, running a close second. *"Jesus, pull out this smoke."*

After lunch a new arrival asked me to fire up his cigarette. I smiled at him gently. "The only fire I've got is the fire of the Holy Spirit. I'll be glad to give you some of that."

Is it loving to remain silent while people poison themselves? By God's grace I want to be more than a picturesque view along life's highway. I want to be a surgeon, not just passing scenery. If I was mixing lemonade with pesticide, I would want someone to make me think.

A smiling fellow from the adjoining 1B2 unit greeted me in the bath area. Told me he's a believer. He knew of our Bible study and said he had started one in 1B2. Praise to Jesus. An answer to prayer! I've thought and prayed about a Bible study with the 60 men in the other end of the building, but they are off limits to us.

Wednesday, March 8.

I've prayed with four more who have come to the Lord. About an hour was spent with a fellow who is descended from a famous evangelist of the last century. He, too, knelt on my bunk to pray the sinner's prayer. I like to have a fellow kneel to evidence sincerity.

Over the weeks I'm finding that my most effective means of winning souls outside the Bible study is sitting down at a table and talking one to one with guys. Often they have just started coming to the group, but haven't made a decision yet. I find out if they know how to be saved, and if they would like me to take a few minutes and explain the plan of salvation. Practically all say, "Yes." I want to believe that this comes across as taking a personal interest in them which I don't have to bother to do. With false assumptions one can make soul saving unnecessarily complex and complicated.

Around 40 have now prayed to receive the Lord since I was put in here. *"Lord, nurture and give them discipline and self control. Keep them from the Evil One. Hold them close in these early days of their spiritual childhood."*

"The Lord preserves all them that love Him . . . " (Psalm 145:20). Evangelists would end up at the funny farm if they thought they bore the responsibility of saving people. Praise God, we are only to be faithful and persistent, leaving the increase to the Almighty.

According to the parable of the sower in Matthew 13, Jesus expects a certain portion of seed to indeed fall on bad, unreceptive soil. Yet that is not to deter us from sowing the seed broadly and reaping all we can. We are to leave regeneration to the Holy Spirit (Titus 3:5).

Jesus is a heart doctor who makes house calls. His diagnosis is always the same for the unsaved person . . . heart surgery (Ezekiel 36:26). He always has an operating room open. You never have to wait. He's the only doctor who can guarantee His work and He never sends a bill (John 6:37, 10:28, Rom. 6:23).

We put the word out that I would be teaching on "Sex, Dating, and Mating" tonight. I hoped it would pull some new men. Praise Jesus! Sixteen came! I shared on the story of Isaac and Rebekah from Genesis 24 and had their attention. They really got into it. Questions popped like firecrackers. I'll give them Part Two tomorrow night.

It's much more peaceful and quiet in here than three or four weeks ago! That, I think, is because there are more Christian witnesses here than before. And from the letters I get, I know that heavy prayer artillery is bombarding this place daily. That's where the battle is won.

Thursday, March 9.

An officer making rounds just stopped by my bunk when I was preparing for Bible study. She looked down at my Bible. I shared my testimony with her. She said she was a churchgoer. I offered a tract, saying, "How about something to read?"

She looked at it and said, "I read that one last week. What else have you got?" I gave her another one.

Part Two of "Sex, Dating, and Mating" drew another big crowd.

Friday, March 10.

The resident turnover seems to be increasing. Two to five new fellows a day arrive, others leave. Bellwood stays rather full though. This obviously means less time to meet and minster to people.

An ill-tempered fellow—not a member of our church—had his portable radio stolen from off his bunk. I expressed my concern to him. It was found in the commode and returned to him. I wonder if the TV would fit in there, too?

Saturday, March 11.

Mary visited me! One hour was the scheduled time, but we were allowed almost two hours. God is good. Such a blessed time together, even though we could only look through the glass and talk through the phones.

Ironically, attorney and pastor visits can be more personal. You can join hands to pray.

What a blessing to have a godly wife. She keeps our home in order. I like to walk in and see her pretty, godly face beaming through the glass.

I shared Jesus with Albert this morning. He's a young, nice looking man, but captured by his own opinions. He's really not open to the Gospel.

I sought to communicate in a gentle but plain way that he was resisting and rejecting God's Word while claiming to believe in God. I ended my ministry effort by offering him Jeremiah 29:13: "And you shall seek Me, and find Me, when you shall search for Me with all your heart."

The most difficult to reach with the saving Gospel of Jesus Christ are those folks from backgrounds with lots of religion and churchanity but little excitement about Jesus as a real person you relate to and interact with. Satan must love religion.

The inquiries of evangelists scared me before I got saved, because down deep I knew I didn't have a satisfactory answer for them. I wasn't really comfortable with my spiritual condition and having it pointed out exposed me. It prompted me to think about my uncertain, spiritual condition. That's uncomfortable for the one trying to avoid Jesus' new birth.

Worldly wisdom says, "Don't discuss religion or politics. You might offend."

Jesus' parting command to us was "Go ye into all the world, and preach the gospel to every creature." (Mark 16:15).

Had a nap after morning Bible study. Paul wasn't there again. He and some others continue in the old habit of staying up most of the night. I reminded the group that we are "children of the day" (1 Thessalonians 5:5).

This afternoon I shared the gospel at length with a new arrival. Buck is here on a morals charge. He's much influenced by a friend who's in a cult.

I posed one of my favorite questions: "Are you happy with the way you're living your life?"

"No," he said.

That question lets one testify against himself. A lost person needs to hear himself admit that he is without the answer to a meaningful life.

I prayed that Buck would soon make the big decision. The great evangelist, Charles Finney said that failing to end your challenge to an unsaved sinner with prayer is to leave the job unfinished.

Eighteen came to evening Bible study—a new high.

Later this evening I played chess to unwind and caught a bit of Christian music.

Before going to sleep, I thought of more provision from God. I've traded for nine boxes of cereal this week. To swap a hamburger for cereal makes two people happy.

Sunday, March 12.

Starting with morning Bible study, I've had a continual flow of pastoral counseling opportunities all day. We get all types in here. I don't always know what they're in for. One new man is a young university drop-out from a big name school. He's a budding golf pro who professes to know the Lord. He said he and his girl friend realized that secular college life was taking them further away from Jesus. So they left school and are thinking of marriage.

I've been wanting to help Jerry, the guy who wants to be my protector, in evangelism. "Would you like to go with me when I visit some unsaved person at their bunk?" I asked.

"Yeah," he shot back, "even if you have to wake me up." Soon after that I woke Jerry and we went to see two new fellows, Cale and Jelly. "You be my silent prayer partner," I told Jerry.

The smoke is better now. *"Thank You, Lord."* The fan in the ceiling above my bunk blows fresh air in and is now being left on for hours at a time, as the weather is getting warmer—82 degrees yesterday.

Why not non-smoking jail units? Many other government buildings already prohibit smoking. What a wonderful time to quit. One inmate said that some Federal prisons provide all the free tobacco one can smoke. That's outrageous.

No call again this Sunday for the Chaplain's worship service. What's going on? Did the preacher not come, or is the system the obstacle? It's hard to get reliable explanations. I've only been twice now in the six Sundays I've been here. I signed up to go to five. I may send a request form to the Major to get an explanation.

Theoretically, inmates can send request forms to a wide variety of officials in the jail system here, from medical, to administrators, to the Chaplain. In most instances, you get a reply or some action, but some requests get no response.

Almost the whole unit has been watching the University of North Carolina-Duke basketball tourney game. Many are now asleep, but they'll rise for supper.

While the snoozing was going on, I had a worthwhile conversation in the bath area with Sonny, whom I talked with previously. His actions suggest that he is unsaved. I shared my testimony and invited him to our evening meeting.

I'm back at my bunk now. Just finished updating my journal. I've got to finish preparation for the evening Bible study. It's challenging to prepare daily talks and Bible studies without reference books, notes, or illustration files. I praise God for my study Bible, though. The Spirit of God is faithful. I teach a good bit of what I've used in the past. They listen and respond. They are so appreciative that Mark and I are here, teaching the precious, simple Word of God.

Praise choruses are new to most of the fellows. I taught them the chorus, "Jesus," at the morning service. Old hymns like "Amazing Grace" are the most popular. We usually sing a mixture.

It's wonderful how the Lord can again and again fill and use this cracked, clay pot. Sometimes it's like I'm a spectator watching it happen. Let Him be glorified.

Christian radio refreshes my soul. The music soothes and the teaching anchors and encourages me.

This solid metal bunk and thin mattress are great for my weak back. It's even firmer than the mattress at home which has boards under it. God is so good, even in small ways. The Word is my foundation here, not only spiritually but physically. I've got four New Testaments and five Bibles spread out under my mattress. Bellwood church is thankful to those who sent them to us. Three is the maximum allowed in one package. The donated Bibles await new church members. We haven't run out of Bibles yet, even though many choose to keep their Bibles upon release. They'll need them when they hit the street. Keep the Bibles coming, folks.

This is about my 40th day. A dramatic release would be wonderful. But let it come in God's time. I'm glad Brenda Roberts is out so she can be ministering. I also trust that God has other plans for the 11 who were arrested with Brenda and me and chose another option than trial. Brenda and I had the same choice. God has different assignments for each of us. No doubt the 11 are being mightily used by God elsewhere. God gets more glory when His servants are greatly outnumbered and victory comes.

I continue to sense the prayers of the saints. I must be in another dimension of ministry here. Things are happening like you read about, but don't normally happen to me. I wonder how much is from the prayers of so many saints and how much is just from being in a truly different, but responsive sub-culture?

I sense God's enabling. They're all looking up to "The Rev," so I must be the strong one, even when I don't feel "up." If I let a bad attitude or critical spirit control me, they might be influenced.

Feelings go up and down like the waves of the sea. To base one's actions on them is often to be at the mercy of anger, fear, and doubt. We get a lot more miles per gallon out of the will than our feelings. The octane may not always be as high, but it is quite adequate and much more stable. Our emotions are often ready to throw in the towel when the road gets bumpy and steep, or our efforts for God go unappreciated by others. *"Jesus, help me to master my feelings."*

I feel fulfilled in ministry here. God's moving is evident and people are responsive to spiritual direction. It's a blessed though temporary situation. It is above all a pastoring experience.

The pastorate, I think, is the most difficult ministry position to fulfill successfully today. Pastors have more diverse problems to deal with than ever before. They have both a challenging and thankless job at times, trying to help people who have yet to commit to a local church or Biblical authority. Too many church hoppers want help, but on their own terms. Some today yield grudgingly to church authority. Until they do, God may just leave them on the shelf.

I feel a cold coming on. I need to nap before the fellows come over for Bible study.

Tuesday, March 14.

We divided the church into five devotion groups with a leader for each. They're supposed to meet together daily to help more fellows jump start their personal devotions. I visited Carl's five-man group today. Carl used a devotional guide that was mailed to us.

It's good to see these young believers confront sins like bad language or making unkind comments to others in the church. Some also asked for forgiveness.

The temptations, the enticements to sin are plentiful, even though this isn't a place for really bad offenders. The TV is probably the worst culprit. It has the effect of a frontal lobotomy on many here, including some of our believers. They sit for hours in front of it. As a missionary friend, Elliot Tepper, commented to me last year, "We think we can handle TV but we can't."

It isn't just the jail. There are Christian homes where the TV runs four, six, even eight hours a day. Yet they cannot find 10 minutes for a family prayer time. Mothers would be outraged if the garbage man came and dumped filth all over their living rooms week after week. Yet we allow perverted TV to dump garbage daily into our minds. The tension-filled filthy soaps, wicked situation comedies, and violent programs aren't edifying to the spirit. The answer isn't legalism, it's godly self control. Purity is the answer. Ninety percent of wisdom is the right use of time.

With these young believers, I try to teach truth and live patience. I don't dilute Scripture's high standards for godliness, while reminding myself that they are brand new babies. I confine my comments on TV to the Bible study.

I'm one of the quieter ones here as social conversations go. I do make it a point to show initiative and welcome new fellows. Sometimes I'll offer to help them put the fitted sheet on their mattress. Getting it on straight can be awkward for someone not used to doing it. Hopefully, friendliness helps answer the big question many have on their minds when entering: "Am I safe here?" They are often quiet as they spy out the land to see what is in store for them—peace, safety, or hostility? Jail veterans know what to expect and tend not to be so quiet and cautious when they enter.

Whatever their experience and demeanor, I pray that I and the brothers in our Bellwood church can minister to their needs.

Chapter 10

"Peanut Butter and Beefsteak"

Wednesday, March 15.

Paul gave me a hug when he left yesterday. Hugs in front of some of these rough old, knuckle-draggers is unusual. Paul has appreciated the church here, though he still has some of the hustler in him. As he left for freedom, I pleaded one more time, "Paul, I'm counting on you going on with the Lord out there. I'm going to be praying for you. You write me. I want to hear how it's going with you. OK?"

Paul gave me that big, disarming smile that communicates, "We're good friends. I won't let you down," and he was gone.

Did he get a big enough dose of Jesus to make it out there? Heaven's roll call will be interesting, with no doubt some surprises and disappointments. *"Lord, help Paul."*

Thursday, March 16.

I didn't get to bed until around 12:30 last night. The 11 p.m. roll call often doesn't come until around 11:20. Occasionally, personal ministry sessions sometimes run until 12:30 or 1 a.m. The day can end on a busy note.

I was up by 5:45 this morning. To continue getting by on such little sleep is another evidence of God's grace. I still try to nap for an hour or more during the day.

6:15 a.m. How touching to see four fellows sitting on bunks near me, meeting with Joe for devotions in **Our Daily Bread.** Two aren't members of our church.

Joe is my next bunk neighbor and one of our church regulars. Lean, lanky, and laid back, this middle-aged brother gives you the impression that he's seen it all before and isn't easily rattled.

My pictures of murdered babies continue to win pro-life converts. If someone is blinded on the baby killing sin, I like to show them reality. The graphic photos of little ones torn limb from limb hit the men hard. I get comments like, "I had no idea that's what happened!" "Man, I could have gone all year without seeing that!" "I'm against that." "Unbelievable!" "This is a good thing you're doing [being in jail for protesting abortion]."

The pictures are a powerful, on-the-spot demonstration of this awful evil which so many "civilized" Americans—even many Christians—allow to continue. Seeing the dramatic and immediate impact that these graphic reflections of reality have on people I am sadly aware of how widely the facts have been covered up by the media. From this I am now impressed to encourage efforts to petition local media outlets not to withhold this valuable information from the public.

Freedom of the press is the public's right to know, not the press's right to print whatever it wants. Daily through the years, each editor and reporter have the choice to print truth or clever, one sided bias masquerading as the "whole" truth.

I can think of only two inmates and two officers who expressed support for abortion out of the many people I've talked with.

Tonight I taught on the Bible's high view of human life. I used Exodus 20:13, Psalm 139:13-14, Jeremiah 1:5. The fellows were quiet and attentive as usual. The church is 15 years in arrears in teaching on the sanctity of human life.

Spent about an hour with each, leading Gilford and Ron to the Lord. Gilford doesn't read. Ron, who lives in southern Georgia, was arrested while drunk and asleep on his own front porch. He came home but didn't have the house key so he went to sleep on the porch. The neighbors saw him and not knowing who he was called the police. They arrested him and found he had violated his probation on a previous sentence. They allegedly held him for ten days until he could be brought here to Atlanta.

"Jesus, there are so many lost folks, so many. I feel I'm only scratching the surface, yet I'm fulfilled in those who do come to You. Part of me wants to minister here and part wants to be out and living normally. Or is this normal living in Christ?"

After 44 days my body is becoming a bit flabby from the need for more exercise. My cough and cold virtually eliminated jogging for the past two weeks.

It's late. I'm tired. *"Move mightily, Jesus. Watch over those who have received You and departed from us."*

Friday, March 17.

After some 45 days here, I'm still getting an average of five letters a day from literally all over the country. With hardly an exception, they have been encouraging and constructive. I did get an unusual negative post card today. But as it was out of the Spirit, with unkind words, I viewed it as further confirmation for my being here.

In jail, one sees how simple our real needs in life are: the Lord, a little food, clothing, housing, and loving support.

The majority of men I witness to in this jail barracks wouldn't know how to be saved if they wanted to. So many confuse religion with conversion. Most look to their own works to save them.

I tell them, "Religion is Satan's counterfeit. Hell will be filled with religious people." But they are only "mouth" Christians, not "heart" Christians. I ask, "Is Jesus number one in your life? Is He in the driver's seat?"

Hardly a day passes that I don't have several opportunities to share my salvation testimony in some way. Jail or other marketplace opportunities to witness exist when I have the boldness to risk.

I tell them how I waited 30 years for God to meet my needs before discovering in Scripture that Christ had "died for the ungodly" and that the ball was in my court.

I tell them that after accepting Jesus, I announced my big decision at a home Bible study. Then I plugged into a Bible-believing church in Knoxville. InterVarsity staffer Wilson Williams became a friend and spiritual father to me and Christian worker Matt Prince fed me on the Word for four years in my new walk of joy in Jesus.

Looking back at my early stumbling and fumbling, I marvel at God's patience. Babies do mess their diapers. I see that I needed both truth and patience. The Lord could have pinched my head off a thousand times and for good reason. He didn't. Glory to His name!

I've never doubted that my decision to follow Jesus was valid and permanent. Nor have I ever regretted making this choice. I do regret that I didn't know how to commit my life to Jesus years earlier. I wish I could have attended Christian primary and secondary schools.

I long for my brothers in Bellwood to become soul winners. My goal for years has been to share Jesus Christ with at least one person every time I go somewhere in my car. It may be sharing a scripture portion or tract—often just leaving something in a phone booth or with a clerk. God promises that His Word will not return to Him "void" (Isaiah 55:11). We are not responsible for the results. We are to be faithful witnesses like Jeremiah who was not at all successful with the hard-hearted crowd God sent him to preach to. He was a prophet but his words did not profit them.

I've told the men here about Uncle John Vassar, a special hero of mine, and one of the greatest American, one-on-one soul winners of the past 200 years. Uncle John was not seminary trained nor ordained. He overflowed with a love and earnestness that came through when witnessing. He camped on the urgency of inviting Jesus into your heart now . . . today! To use the old Puritan phrase, he "pressed in" with the sinner. He once met Ulysses S. Grant and held on to the president's hand until he could finish questioning him about the new birth.

Uncle John labeled himself "the Good Shepherd's dog," hunting up lost sheep. He traveled from coast to coast, talking to an average of 40 families a day. After greeting a stranger, his immediate question was, "My friend, would you kindly permit me to ask, have you been born again?" If the answer was unconvincing, Uncle John would say, "Let's see what God has to say about that." Then he would turn to John 3:3 in his well-worn Bible.

Somewhere down the path of humanistic psychology, affluence, and the old liberal God-is-love-not-judgment line, many Christians have lost their stomach for old fashioned soul winning. We spray paint sin and treat repentance like a backwoods cousin.

By contrast, in these urgent, last days of human history before the Lord returns the libertines, evolution-minded educators, new age mediums, sexually explicit rock music, and anti-Christian TV shows are certainly not bashful about getting their messages across. They don't lack boldness. If we are not straightforward about our convictions we'll be about the only ones who aren't.

"For I am not ashamed of the gospel of Christ: for it is the power of God unto salvation to every one that believeth; to the Jew first, and also to the Greek" (Romans 1:16).

By His grace, I intend to be a fork in the road causing men to choose for or against Jesus Christ. I don't want there to be any doubt in heaven, earth, or hell about where I stand. GLORY TO HIS NAME! I'LL SHOUT IT OUT FOR ALL TO HEAR: ALL NEED TO BE SAVED AND SAVED TODAY!!!!

Walter, a bleak-faced fellow, got into a financial scrape in his business. He got the bunk above me. He, like me, comes from a mainline religious background. Talking with him revealed only some distant date that he joined the church and was baptized. I don't sense that his "joining" is really meaningful to him, though. It evidently was not life changing. He doesn't seem to see Jesus as a real person with whom he is interacting hour by hour. The Bible says that Christ is the groom and His church is the bride. I don't see evidence that Wally has that vital marriage relationship with Jesus Christ.

Walter has the ability to sleep through the Bible study and the robust singing as the church meets on the bunk below him. The Devil works through such sleepiness and lack of discipline.

I explained to Walter that "religion kills. It is a counterfeit for the real thing. Will sitting in a garage day after day make you an automobile, Walter? Will going in a hen house make you a chicken? Neither will walking in a church house make you a Christian. Going to church is what a Christian does. It is not what a Christian is.

"One isn't saved by joining a church, be it mine or five others. New life comes only when you invite Jesus to come in and take control of your life. Only Jesus saves."

Walter did show some interest. The other day he called me aside, saying, "I'd like to talk."

I shared my heart. "Walter, I really think you are running from the Lord. Is that why things aren't coming together as you would like?"

He didn't disagree, but said only, "I need to do some thinking." Now he's gone. He got released just a little while ago.

Praise God that He has not overlooked any of the needed tools to be effective witnesses. A gentle attitude and right spirit can be the difference between coming across as surly and abrasive rather than with firm, earnest, loving concern.

Joe, who's been attending the Bible study for leaders, was also told he could "pack it up." Before leaving, he testified that the Bible study was a good experience for him.

C.J., the surly fellow who had his portable radio lifted and dumped in the toilet, just got his long awaited good news. A short, steamy, muscular fellow, C.J. has been here about as long as I have. He's from up north. He's shown no interest in spiritual things and expresses his rebellion against the Lord verbally. He curses con-

tinually with fire in his eyes. He's been among the most resistant
to the gospel, never attending our Bible study.

As C.J. was getting ready to exit to freedom, I walked over and
put my arm around him. "C.J., Jesus loves you, cares about you,
and wants you to let Him wash away your sins today. You're not
happy the way you're living your life, are you?" He answered with
a quiet "no." *"Lord, work on C.J."*

Another fellow who has resisted the Gospel and our church
confesses (brags?) of having stolen 40 cars in a month. He, like
others, probably wants a free trip on Jesus' train to Heaven, but
knows he can't bring along his suitcase of wrongdoing. Hopefully,
this boy will not someday discover that heaven can't be broken into
like an automobile.

In a world of shallowness and fashionable sin, I find that hurting
folks respect plain, country honesty. Truth offered soberly touches
something deep inside the sinner that nothing else will. He already
is convicted of sin and needs to have the truth confirmed, explained, crystallized. I see Jesus, Peter, and Paul doing this consistently with sinners in the New Testament.

Who wants an attorney who won't tell you the risk factor in a big
legal matter? Who has confidence in a dentist who won't be honest
when he discovers a root canal problem? We need to know what's
causing the hurt in our lives.

Professionalism begins with evaluating a patient's problem ob-
jectively and then presenting a diagnosis. Withholding truth is not
caring. Hiding the life-saving medicine is not love.

You can go to a quack and get squirted with froth and foam. That
doesn't help. Our Creator God made the human heart as a recep-
tacle for the two-prong plug of love and truth. The key is balance.
Denying truth prevents deliverance. "You shall know the truth,
and the truth shall make you free" (John 8:32). "Righteousness and
justice are the foundation of Thy throne; loving-kindness and truth
go before Thee" (Psalm 89:14, NASV). "All the paths of the Lord
are loving-kindness and truth to those who keep His covenant and
His testimonies" (Psalm 25:10, NASV).

Our 3:30 p.m. leaders' Bible study has four right now. We're
looking at Philippians 2:1-11. Christ's humility should lead us to
be humble also.

These leaders are eager learners, especially Carl. Since Mark led
him to the Lord about two weeks ago, Carl has been a regular

member. He catches on quickly and soaks up Bible concepts like a sponge. He passes out the song sheets and is enthusiastic about learning to lead a Bible study. I see leadership potential in Carl.

This new convert is around 22, always cheerful and smiling. Carl's fun-loving and likes to cut up. He's muscular and does pushups along with several others nightly in a sort of contest. Two hundred push-ups, in sets of 20, is not uncommon in the barracks.

Wiley is a short, middle-aged fellow, with a face longer than his years. He seems to carry much of the weight of the world on his shoulders. He's been coming to Bible study for only a week or two.

We prayed for Wiley before he went to court today. He came back to pack up and tell us, "I got off on 'time served'"—meaning the sentence was reduced to the time he had already spent in jail. "Prayer is the reason," he declared.

"I've got a drinking problem," Wiley admitted, "and I need some friends." We try to give each church member a warm sendoff. We wish them well and pledge our prayers.

We also prayed for Sam before he went to court. He got probation and AA rehabilitation. God is moving in power and mercy in many hearts.

I see so many here with alcohol related problems. I wish the beer and liquor ads would tell this side of the story. This isn't quite the gusto some thought they were grabbing. If the beer is less filling, the jail cells are filled.

Mark continues as a faithful co-teacher. The primary principles that we teach are so simple, yet so foreign to most church members. Teachers had best not become tired of these basics. Nine times out of ten when a young disciple doesn't go on with Jesus, it's because he has failed to:

(1) Feed his new nature on the "beefsteak" of the Bible that grows a strong inner man able to resist temptation and sin. Psalm 1:2, 119:9. Pure, godly living is not an optional extra like tinted windows or rear seat speakers. It's normality for the committed believer.

(2) Or maintain his prayer fellowship with Jesus. This is like a deep sea diver's need to keep oxygen flowing through his air hose from above. Genesis 19:27, Mark 1:35, 14:38.

(3) Or separate himself from old habits, hangouts, and friends that pull him down spiritually. God says, "Wherefore come out from among them, and be ye separate, saith the Lord, and touch not the unclean thing; and I will receive you . . . " (2 Corinthians 6:17). Sheep hang around with other sheep, not goats.

(4) Or find and become part of a good church (Hebrews 10:25). Lone ranger Christians tend to be overly critical, independent, often with a faulty concept of love and commitment. They lack ministry involvement. God may put them on the shelf.

I tell the fellows that the absence of any of these basics of the Christian walk is a blinking caution light warning of problems ahead. An engine must be hitting on all cylinders to get up the hills. If the foundation of the new believer's spiritual house is not firmly established, whatever follows will suffer and sooner or later probably fall.

Supper time. We had baked fish with a red sauce, mashed potatoes, slaw, and pecan pie. I traded all but the slaw for two boxes of Cheerios to be served in the morning. I can get peanut butter from the commissary. I've just discovered that peanut butter with slaw on it for crunchiness is good. I'm now eating one or two of these sandwiches most every day to replace the food I trade or give away. Like Bible "beefsteak" for the growing Christian, I'm finding peanut butter sandwiches to be a staple.

An officer just noted how quiet this barracks is compared to a month ago. Praise God for the calming effect which His Word is having. "Great peace have they which love Thy law: and nothing shall offend them" (Psalm 119:165).

11:00 p.m. I'm waiting for the three officers on the graveyard shift to arrive and have head count so I can hit the hay. It's chilly in here tonight. I may wear my longjohns and flannel pajamas. The fresh air fan above my bed is blowing in very cool air.

12:15 a.m. The officers made their head count. I'm still ministering. Just had a precious bedtime prayer and talk with Pete. He's a cheerful guy with a bubbly disposition. Lucifer's liquor got him in here.

Pete commented, "I'm not sure I would leave now if I could. This Bible teaching is what I need." Pete was saved just 10 days ago.

I'm finding that seven or eight out of ten of the men here will discuss spiritual things the first time I meet them. Many lonely souls are waiting for someone to speak to them of lasting, heavenly matters. Did not God the Creator make us to think and speak of such even on a daily basis? Asking earnestly with a loving heart opens doors to lonely souls. I want to minister in the emergency room of men's souls to deep and eternal needs. Souls are too dear to stay in the "play room."

This really has become an incredible, short term missions trip. I would choose to go through this experience again. God is faithful in crisis. His grace is sufficient.

Chapter 11

"More Joy in Heaven"

Saturday, March 18.

Lunch today was ideal for a diet like mine: boiled potatoes, pinto beans, turnip greens, corn bread, cookie, and lemonade. It's about what I would have had at home, aside from home cooking. Corn bread is a special favorite here. Fellows will even trade cake for it.

It's my time again to help with clean up. Four men each day are assigned to sweep, wipe tables, mop the floor, and clean the bath area. My turn rolls around every two weeks or so. This is the only work detail we have here.

Even so, some shirk this little 20-minute detail, or hire a substitute with a candy bar.

Mail call. One letter was from a former Bellwood brother, Keith, who rededicated his life to Christ here about a month ago. He's doing well. He's witnessing, selling cars, and has seen two other brothers who were here. *"Thank You, Lord, for giving us fruit that remains."*

The officer who commented on the quietness stopped again at my bunk to chat briefly while making her rounds of the room. I gave her the Scripture portion, "Help From Above."

After the officer left, I had the opportunity to sit at a table and share Jesus with Tully, a new arrival. We got acquainted, then I launched right into the gospel: "Tully, are you interested in spiritual things?"

"I used to go church," he offered.

"Do you know which way you would go if you died tonight?"

"I hope I'd go to Heaven."

"Are you 100 percent certain which way you'd go or just hoping?"

"Nobody can be certain, can they?"

"I'm certain. In fact I've got a written guarantee that's even better than a Midas Muffler lifetime warranty!"

Seeing no falloff in interest, I kept going. "God promises in His Word that one can know for certain he is saved and going to Heaven. Does God lie?"

"No."

"Tully, would you like me to show you a four-step plan of salvation from the Bible? I can tell you how you can be saved and know for certain you're going to Heaven."

He nodded "yes."

I opened my Bible and presented the first step: "God loves you." Tully understood that.

Step number two is man's problem, sin. I took some time on that. Francis Schaeffer has said that if he had an hour to speak to humanity, he would spend the first 45 minutes on sin. If sin is not very important, neither is salvation from sin.

"Tully, now that we agree with Romans 3:23 that all have sinned, please read Romans 6:23."

He squinted at the verse and read slowly and aloud. "For the wages of sin is death; but the gift of God is eternal life through Jesus Christ our Lord."

"Tully, what is a wage?"

"It's a salary."

"Yes, it is our paycheck. And when I 'work' at sin, what does this verse say I will receive?"

"Death."

Tully was all ears as I forged ahead. "Satan is a faithful paymaster. He pays his employees on time. If I've been working at alcohol addiction for five years, the paycheck could be death by drunk driving. If I've been doing drugs, Satan says, 'Here's your salary, death by overdose.' If I'm chasing after wild women or homosexuality, the payment can be death by a jealous husband or AIDS. Sins are bullets in Satan's gun. We can't work at sin and not expect to get paid."

Tully's non-verbal communication suggested no resistance to the truth he was hearing. He wanted to hear more, so I continued. "What is sin?"

"It's what we do, I guess."

I extended my hand to clutch some imaginary object. "What causes this old hand to grab things it shouldn't? Is it the skin or bone that causes my hand to sin? If I cut off my hand would that stop my sinning?"

"No," Tully slowly offered, "it's in the heart."

"You're absolutely right. So sin is more than what we do with our hands or feet or eyes watching what they shouldn't, isn't it? How do we get rid of sin then? How do we get it out of the heart and mind?"

"You've got to change the heart, I reckon."

"Right, but now how do we do that? Can you change your own heart? If I can stop my sinning 100 percent, why haven't I already done it? We say we've been trying hard, doing the best we can, but yet we still sin. So what's the answer?"

"I don't know," he confessed.

"God is holy, Tully. Not one sin will ever enter heaven. How can I get to heaven if I've sinned even once? What would heaven be like if everyone in Atlanta went to heaven and took their sins with them?"

Tully's mouth relaxed in a grin. "It would be about as bad as it is here."

"So what's the answer?" I pressed.

"I don't know."

I handed him my Bible and asked that he read Romans 5:6. I put my finger over the last word of the verse. "What does it say here—that Christ died for the 'godly' or the 'ungodly?'" I sat back and waited for his answer to this big 'exam' question. Had he understood what I had been trying to get across?

"He died for the ungodly," Tully ventured.

"Right!" I said, complete with arm gestures. "If we were already godly, why would Christ need to come from heaven to die for us? And besides we saw in Romans 3:23 that there are no godly people because 'all have sinned.'" After looking at Romans 3:10 and Isaiah 64:6 to further nail this down, I pointed him to the cross. "Tully, if salvation is indeed a free gift from Christ, how can we pay for something that He has already paid for? That would be like paying for a Christmas or birthday gift, wouldn't it? To pay for any gift makes it no longer a free gift. Right? If I'm earning my way to heaven then that makes me my own Savior, doesn't it? Why would I need someone to come all the way from heaven and die for me if I'm already saving myself? I don't need two Saviors do I? Who is my Savior?"

I asked him to read Titus 3:5 from the NASV: "He saved us, not on the basis of deeds which we have done in righteousness, but according to His mercy . . . . "

Tully came to understand that (1) he needed to be saved, (2) he could not save himself, (3) God had provided for his salvation, (4) Jesus is able to save and keep eternally. I concluded this lengthy presentation by asking, "Tully, does all this make sense to you? Is the Holy Spirit whispering to your heart that you're hearing truth from God or did I maybe make this up?"

"Oh, it's from God," he confirmed quickly.

"OK, so if the Holy Spirit is speaking to you, is it just to entertain you, or do you think He wants you to act on it?"

"To act," he said.

"Do you have any questions? Is it clear? I don't want to talk you into anything. It's a big decision. Are you ready?"

"I'm ready."

"Would you like to pray now and invite Jesus to come in and sit on the throne of your life as your Lord and Savior? Let Him become your teacher, boss, captain, coach, and friend. Is that what you want?"

"Yes," he said promptly.

We walked from the table to my bunk where we both knelt and I led him in the sinner's prayer. He opened his eyes and I trust began seeing things in a new light.

"Thank You, Lord. Watch over this new sheep."

Nine p.m. Sixteen came to evening Bible study. This is amazing, since five of our brethren were released this week. I would not have guessed that this many fellows here would attend two daily meetings of an hour to an hour-and-a-half each. Perhaps God wants Bellwood to be an interstate rest area where needy men can pull off the highway of life, get spiritual air in their tires, and continue on.

We agreed that if Mark and I got released unexpectedly, Carl would take over as leader of the group. Carl says he would continue on with the Bible study.

Study materials are no problem now. We've got two or three Bible study guides from friends in South Carolina.

I made a call to rural Tennessee tonight. I called my spiritual mentor, Wilson Williams. This red-headed, raw-boned, godly brother is a down-home, dirt-in-the-cuff family man who loves Jesus and can teach the Bible. He's a seminary trained farm fellow who still lives and works in a remote setting.

Wilson was delighted to learn about happenings in Bellwood. He recalled our prayer some time back that God would give me an increased ministry. What a treasured friend and advisor Wilson is.

Mary and I are blessed to have some warm family ties and a few close friends. It's well worth the effort to maintain these ties over the years.

Chapter 12

"Easter in Jail"

Palm Sunday, March 19.

I was denied permission to attend the Chaplain's service again, along with our brethren here. I don't understand why. The two I did attend were excellent evangelistic services led by lay evangelists who gave altar calls. One declared: "Taxes didn't build this jail—sin did."

The newspaper today had a story and a picture of a hundred picketers at a local abortion facility yesterday. The picketing was peaceful, as usual.

Abortion is, of course, just a knot on the log of sin. To get someone saved can give a person an appreciation for God's view of human life. Thus evangelism in the right places could be an effective pro-life activity. Sidewalk counseling with pregnant young women takes some of the same heart and courage as personal evangelism.

More new "guests" joined us today. Initial conversation with new men often revolves around the circumstances which brought them here and how quickly they can get out. Right away they want to phone out for help or borrow a pen to write the pre-trial release program.

I listen to inmates' stories with reserve. Some seem to proclaim their evil exploits more than show grief and sorrow over them. Drugs or alcohol are often involved even though not mentioned. I want to give a fellow the benefit of the doubt. I want to be a good listener, while assuming that some stories are apt to be overly subjective or fictional.

I'm realizing that it's possible to get two versions of why a person was arrested . . . from the same person. You hear the first account when they arrive. Later after they become involved in our Bellwood church, or perhaps have time to think about it, you get a more

balanced rendition in which they accept more responsibility for
their actions. Reminds me of the old country fellow who said he
would "explain" a story five or six different ways to keep from
telling a lie.

Some stories are told in a way that touches the heart. You want
them to be true. One fellow said he was arrested for urinating in
an alley. Another said he loaned his girl friend $200 and held her
VCR as collateral. Instead of repaying, she claimed he stole the
VCR. Another said he was picked up for improper lane change.
Another blamed his incarceration on a property dispute with his
wife.

I've decided that most fellows that are here probably should be.
Even when the rest of the story surfaces, it often seems that
discretion or Biblical principles were violated. The "innocent"
victim no longer seems so innocent.

Yet some of these fellows remain in jail because they don't have
money for bail. Is that presuming guilt until proven innocent? I'm
not an attorney, but that doesn't seem like justice to me. A person
could be locked up on a relatively minor offense until his trial three
months later.

Behavior speaks louder than words in here. You have a few fast
talkers that can quickly play on your sympathy to get what they
want. Over time you can discern motives but during initial conversations it isn't easy. Still, I'd rather err on the generous side.

I wonder if God doesn't say at times, "OK, you won't respect my
laws and rights, so I'll violate your 'rights'? I'll allow you to be
unjustly arrested and even held for weeks without being charged."

Is God more interested in our rights than our righteousness?
Does God say, "You need time to lie down in green pastures and
think about how you're living your life and running from Me?"
Certainly this would not account for all the situations here, yet God
can use each one, bringing good out of evil.

I tell the men in our Bible studies that "How soon will I be
released?" is not the only question they should ask, but also: "Why
did God allow me to be here?" "What does God want me to become
or understand, while I'm here?" "Does God have me here to hear
the gospel?"

I'm convinced that God sends most to Bellwood for exposure to
a clear gospel presentation so they can be born again. "Now is the
day of salvation" (2 Corinthians 6:2, NASV).

In the Bible study tonight we continued going through the events
leading up to the first Easter. I shared from Matthew 21. This is

such a peak-to-valley passage—from the multitudes accepting Jesus as their King on His "Palm Sunday" triumphal entry into Jerusalem, to His rejection by the Jewish authorities.

After "church" tonight, I did some reflecting on my own resurrection new-life attitudes. I recalled a flash of anger when a non-believer, who had not returned my newspaper as agreed, came to borrow another one. I tried to excuse my action by thinking of the numerous times I've given out stationery, envelopes, stamps, newspapers, lotion, and pens which I haven't gotten back.

I can be grudging with my pens. Some fellows who have been here for weeks will repeatedly borrow a pen from me rather than buy one from the commissary for thirty-five cents. "Lord, it would be a lot easier to keep a good attitude, if these people wouldn't borrow my pens so often."

The thought comes—no doubt from the Holy Spirit: Are the souls here not worth thirty-five cents each? I'm shamed. The little foxes have stolen the grapes (Song of Solomon 2:15). My old nature is exposed but not dead. Could it not have stayed at home just this once?

Life here could be viewed as an experiment. What will a man do when his food and shelter needs are met and he is free to spend his time any way he chooses, hour after hour, day after day?

Will he seek God less or more? Will the same man use this time as a spiritual retreat or follow his old unsaved nature?

How closely related a disciplined daily schedule is to our daily meeting with the resurrected Jesus. It seems that the natural inclination of men here is to maximize pleasure and minimize pain. Some unsaved men play cards and look at TV four to twelve hours every day. Sleep, reading, and eating gobble up the rest of their time. Some read novels by the hour. Why will an unsaved man often spend more time reading the thoughts of man than a saved man will in reading the thoughts of God?

10:20 p.m. I could go out on an appeal bond, but I continue to remain because God wants me here. I have peace about staying.

I'm certainly not suffering in this round-the-clock recreation room. I recall though that someone said, "When suffering is given purpose it ceases to be suffering."

We have the seeds of real Christian fellowship in our Bellwood church. The brothers are beginning to give food items to others as they learn their favorite dishes. Even with my swapping I still give away food almost daily.

Genuine Christian *koinonia* reminds me of old fashioned, country, front porch friendship. Friendship is at a low ebb in our culture. It has gone from leisurely front porch rocking with neighbors to a passing wave of the hand. Not that table conversations are a Christian invention but appreciation for using meal time to share and develop relationships is not widely appreciated among many here. Here meals are eaten quickly and in silence. It's difficult to get a casual discussion going with most of the unsaved. It's a challenge to find mutually agreeable discussion topics. They probably talk a bit more when "Brother Kerr," the minister, is not at their table however.

Monday, March 20.

Mark said, "We need to pray for deliverance for a guy. This older fellow, who bunks near me took 19 showers yesterday. He lacks self-confidence and doesn't seem very stable. Some of the men apparently talked him out of his commissary items. One of our brothers tried to help him. Another gave him dry underwear."

This older gentlemen also began crying for no apparent reason in a Bible study. I stopped and said, "We're going to pray for you right now." Heads bowed in the group as we reached out in prayer and love.

I enjoyed a morning visit from a pastor friend, Bob Lake. A chaplain's aide spotted me leaving the visitation booth. He was responding to the form I had sent in requesting information on why several of us in Bellwood hadn't been permitted to regularly attend the Sunday Chaplain's services. Services weren't held on March 5 and 12," he explained. "That is why your name wasn't called out to attend on one of those days. Yesterday, 120 signed up but the chapel only holds about 70 or so."

That partially explains it. But why can't they hold several services on Sunday to accommodate all of the people in this 2100-person resident facility who would want to attend?

Mail call! I got 51 letters and Easter cards, and it isn't even Easter yet. One came from my Mary dated the 17th:

". . . It certainly was good to hear your voice yesterday. I get anxious to talk with you after about a day and a half—I can wait that long. The

sound of your voice lets me know how confident
you are of being there. Questions are starting
to come up in my mind more now—March has been
longer than February. I don't say this to get
you concerned, but just to be aware that I am
feeling the effects of your being away . . . "

I am reminded that my loved one at home is paying a price. Her
life has also been interrupted by this experience. First Peter, which
I've been reading lately, links commitment to cost. My Mary will
receive heaven's award.

Two women shared their experience with abortion:

Dear Brother Kerr:

When I was 17 and not a Christian, I went to
an abortuary to find out if I was expecting.
When they informed me that I was, they insisted
it would be better for me to have an abortion
because I was not married and very young. Even
then, I knew within my heart that killing unborn
babies was wrong. Thanks be to God I knew better
and what Satan meant for bad God turned into
good.

I'm now 30 years old and have been married to
my husband 10 years. Next year he will finish
seminary and enter full-time ministry. Our Lord
is so good—I just praise Him for loving me when
no one else did, including myself.

God bless you and know that you are not alone!

Your Sister in Him

Dear Rev. Kerr:

I had an abortion in 1971 before Roe v. Wade.
I'm almost certain that if people like you had
been outside of that clinic, my baby would be a
happy, healthy 17-year-old today. Things did not
turn out well for me, but because of people like
you others are willing to listen. I will pray
for you and your release. I am also trying to
do all I can to help aborted women and to turn
the [Supreme Court's] abortion decision around.

```
Sincerely,

A lady in Pennsylvania
```

How wonderful to know that Jesus is still in the forgiving business for ladies like this. He really does care. When David confessed his sin of sexual immorality and murder, God forgave him. Any man or woman with guilt from any participation in any abortion can invite God in to forgive this sin and every sin. Powerful forgiveness waits the one who is ready to repent and turn to Jesus Christ. Because it may take years for the hurt to heal, even after the guilt is gone, that dramatizes how hideous abortion is. It can be easier for God to forgive an abortion than for the repentant mother to forgive herself and fill the void.

If aborturaries really care about women why are so many not warned about these known, not uncommon, long term consequences?

All the grief over an aborted child will not bring it back. A mother need not be crushed by carrying needless, heavy weights, when she can roll them off on Jesus. "Come unto me all ye that labor and are heavy laden, and I will give you rest. Take my yoke upon you, and learn of me; for I am meek and lowly in heart: and ye shall find rest unto your souls" (Matthew 11:28, 29). God's strong shoulders carry burdens better than ours do.

Tuesday, March 21.

A cool, rainy spring day outside, but damp and chilly in here. No heat is on. With many of us going around wrapped in our blankets, the scene resembles an Indian look-a-like contest.

We are issued only one blanket each. Any extra blankets are confiscated when discovered. We can have long johns, but not coats.

I came up with a blanket making idea which I explained to a deputy friend who liked it. Simply spread newspapers between your sheet and blanket. You can have a three, six, ten-page blanket, or whatever. Add pages to taste. Don't stir.

It works fine. The papers stay in place and just two or three layers seem to hold heat. The covering is noisy and does feel a bit stiff. It's like being a peanut in the shell, but far preferable to being cold.

Wednesday, March 22.

Puddles of water were scattered around the floor when we awoke. Condensation from the walls is a problem here when it rains. Strange.

You can look out the high windows by climbing up on a double bunk. The windows are thick, honeycombed glass and have bars. Eight or nine feet up you get a rather clear view of some grass, another building, and the street. It would be nice to be outside, even if it is raining.

I just counseled with a Bellwood church member who was in a shoving match with a non-church fellow. Unfortunately, the non-church fellow is not open to resolving the problem. He has gotten into several scrapes, which he evidently started. Fighting is recreation for him it appears.

My personal witnessing zeal is waning right now. I only have so much energy. The pastoring is taking so much of my energy and time.

I encouraged the brethren to do more witnessing, but the Holy Spirit must ultimately give the desire. Guilt and nagging are not gifts of the Spirit. Being a live role model as Jesus was before His disciples is so much better. A few seemed to pick up on it.

Mark and I talked about responses of various members we've seen go through the church in the past seven weeks. With such constant contact with the same people, it's hard to hide one's real self for long. We identified and agreed on several who appeared to be like the rocky soil in the Parable of the Sower of Matthew 13.

We're praying for these Bellwood alumni. *"Jesus, keep them from the Evil One."*

I want to believe that ministry seeds are being planted in men in this barracks who are not in our church. We Christians are very much on display here. Others hear the singing, they see us meeting faithfully. Unfortunately, they can be quick to point out shortcomings of our members. I reminded one non-believer that Christians aren't perfect, but just forgiven. We are not perfected yet. There is a growth process after one is born again. It can take years to pull all the weeds sin has planted in our lives. "But Tom, when you and I stand before God on Judgment Day, we're only going to have to give account for one person. Who do you think that will be?" He knew.

Now and then an unsaved man will bring up the recent problems of the TV ministers. The barber shop spectators have gotten much mileage out of this, and often go unchallenged. We do the unsaved man no favor to let him continue to think he is on the winning side.

Neither scorn nor hypocrisy need walk off the court thinking the
match has been won.

I find the scandals of the TV preachers to be an excellent bridge
into the Gospel. I appreciate such an opportunity. "Yes," I say,
"what they did is a disappointment, but it's also a powerful
reminder that God isn't going to overlook anyone's sin. And if we
won't deal with it, He will.

"Have you ever done anything that you wouldn't want shown on
television? I know I have. Who hasn't? Right now God is graciously
giving each person the opportunity to turn from his sins. Do you
think it would be wiser to repent and let Jesus wash all your sins
away now or have them exposed on Judgment Day television. . . .
Have you done that yet? . . . . My friend, would you like to do it
now?"

"Therefore having overlooked the times of ignorance, God is now
declaring . . . that all everywhere should repent" (Acts 17:30,
NASV)

I was reminded of my own shortcomings today. I was sharing a
devotional on my bunk with two young, new church members,
Kevin and Ron. In the midst of this a Cuban named Ramon burst
in on us asking for something. With some irritation I informed him,
"We are praying right now!"

After supper Ramon was waiting for me at the foot of my bunk
to talk. He asked simply, "You're a real Christian, why did you get
mad at me?" This-not-so spiritual minister apologized to the non-
believer. I was very tempted to qualify my apology, pleading guilty
to a lesser offense by mentioning his interruption, but did not. The
little foxes continue to nibble at the grapes.

Instances like this remind me that I, too, have clay feet. I'm not
somehow above all the challenges of daily life here that confront
others, saved and unsaved.

*Lord, forgive me for my shortcomings. Forgive me for getting
mad at the man who interrupted. I need your grace and mercy,
Jesus.*

In tonight's Bible study we had a praise time. We normally begin
with several hymns and Scripture choruses from song sheets sent
us. We have only the single hymnal we asked for at the Chaplain's
service. We had to tear the covers off first, as no hardbacked books
are allowed in here. Not even Bibles.

Leading the worship can sometimes be like pulling teeth to draw out joy and praise. At times there is a heaviness and I almost feel like I'm singing a solo. It takes time to scrape all the Devil's mud off the heart.

Reading the Word, singing aloud, shouting out loud, and petitioning are some of the worship activities encouraged in the Word of God. It's a glorious, all-consuming endeavor, honoring our wonderful Lord. For us it's uplifting, strengthening the inner man.

Late evening thoughts on separation and holy living in a noisy jail barracks:

I'm glad that I'm ignorant on some things, like current movie stars' names and revellings; the latest dirty jokes that are making the rounds; the newest, suggestive dance step; and other fleshly fads. How freeing! How good to be wonderfully out of touch, not knowing or caring about these and other lures.

"Holy" means separated. To have the "Holy" Spirit is to have His view of separation from worldliness. Romans 1:4 says the "Spirit of holiness" has declared Jesus to be "the Son of God with power."

Can one walk towards the world and move closer to Jesus at the same time? The war between flesh and spirit is a most neglected topic in our materialistic culture. I heard a wise pastor say that he had to give up some hobbies because they cost him too much time. Not that they were immoral, but just too consuming.

Hobbies and trivia consume our valuable, disposal time. Many gadgets can eat up time. They can become the Christian's "alcohol." The spirit says pray. The flesh says play.

We spend years seeking ways to accommodate the spirit without having to deprive our flesh. We want it both ways. Who wins the fight when family prayer time arrives after supper? Bible reading or TV?

Flesh vs. spirit is the silent, daily struggle we all wrestle with. I am no perfected expert, but only a fellow struggler.

The great evangelist Charles Finney said that if you want to have revival, but not convict anybody, preach on sin, but don't mention any of the sins of the congregation.

Be thankful for the pastor who doesn't know all the latest fads and dresses a bit out of style. Such men seem to be a dying breed. Maybe we can learn something from such a shepherd. John the Baptist was molded in the wilderness furnace, not in the window of fashion. The man who speaks for God will be focused on something higher than passing do-dads. A nation will rise no higher than its pulpits.

Thursday, March 23.

Ministry in Bellwood is rewarding. The men continue to express appreciation for my being here, for the church, and teaching from Mark and me. Mark still teaches in the morning and I teach in the evening.

Just to look around this drab environment and see men pouring over God's precious Word is rewarding. If that won't light your fire, maybe the wood is wet.

I never know what will happen from one situation to the next. A new resident asked, "Would you write a letter to my wife for me? She had me arrested for abusing her." I agreed to write the letter.

We filled the two-page letter with warm and endearing words. It was smooth. He wanted her to get him out of jail and let him come back to the house.

We were just about finished when it became clear that he had not been honest with me. His "wife" was only his girlfriend. He was using me to patch up a sexually immoral relationship. I was incensed! I immediately tore up the letter, rebuking him (Proverbs 24:25). "Ministers," I declared, "don't promote evil. You're playing games with God!"

"Would you at least give me some paper to write her on?" he brashly persisted.

"No," I said firmly. "We are not to join others in their sin."

He claims to be a backslidden believer, but said earlier that he would go to hell if he died tonight. I hosed him off with the Word of God from 1 Corinthians 6:9-11.

He comes across as a hustler, a smoothy. Both Psalms and Proverbs encourage hard words for the hardhearted and solace for the seeker. I felt his behavior called for the former. *"Reach him, Lord."*

"Winking at sin leads to sorrow; bold reproof leads to peace" (Proverbs 10:10, LB).

Yesterday, I was lying on my bunk reading praise verses and praising Him when my focus changed. I began pleading and petitioning God to move powerfully and shake the pillars of power and authority in Atlanta. Immediately, I heard a single, resounding clap of thunder. The timing was perfect. It was the first thunder I've heard since being here.

Such a privileged, blessed, unthankful people we Americans are. *"Forgive us, Lord."'*

Praying for our country reminds me of the story of the infantry officer whose encampment was being overrun by the enemy. He wanted them defeated so much that he radioed for the heavy artillery to shell his own position. Does praying for revival and repentance in America at whatever the cost mean asking what the brave officer ordered?

"Lord God, I'm thankful for your offer to spare Sodom, if only 10 righteous people could be found. I do sense that prayer and praying people are coming forth for America. Is this your way, Lord? Is it sufficient to heal our death rattle cough?

"Dear God, I hurt for our land and long to see unrighteousness gone from us. I long for safe streets, murder to cease, traditional values in schools, full churches, and empty taverns. I long for godly people in high places. Oh Jesus, I'm describing what only You and the millennium can bring in fullness. But revival we must have soon. You want us to pray Lord, . . . we're praying.

"Move, Holy Spirit in power. Lord, forgive me for at times taking for granted the wonderful evangelism and pastor-teaching opportunities I have here daily. I can't do everything, but I can impact my exciting world right here. May I be found faithful when You return."

Good Friday, March 24.

On this day which Christians celebrate as the anniversary of Christ's crucifixion, sin still flourishes. Would-be Christian counselors would be in hog heaven in Bellwood. Divorce, wife beating, drug and alcohol addiction, aggressiveness, violent behavior, unforgiveness, lust, stealing, bitter spirits, rebellion, strange doctrines, and more are apt to be found. Pull up a chair and take your pick. You find it all in here.

Private and public rehab centers can't fix what's wrong with many people here. They don't have an instrument long enough to reach deep into the soul and spirit as Jesus can. They might bring a tear to the eye, but they can't cleanse and change the heart. They are elephant hunting with a BB gun.

All the humanistic therapists can do is shoot them full of pills and zombie juice. That only masks or distorts the problem. It delays deliverance. They don't have any supernatural medicine from heaven. No wonder the long term cure rates of most secularists are so low. Deliverance is from the Lord.

The sinful individual needs to have the curtains pulled back and to see the spiritual warfare as it is. I deal plainly and openly with people as I would want them to do with me, if I were lost. A man's soul is too important to just play ring-around-the-rosy. He needs saving truth presented with sweetness and love.

I bare my heart to these souls: "Jesus cares about you. The Devil's been trying to kill you, hasn't he? Liquor is the Devil's handshake. Drugs are hell's front porch. Does the Devil have his foot on your neck? Has sin had its hand in your back pocket? Haven't you had enough? Wouldn't you like to kick the Devil out today?"

I make it real. Some tell of close calls, confirming that Satan has been trying to kill them. They know I'm talking about reality.

One must deal with his sin before the cross before he can be saved by the cross. Diagnosis precedes treatment. Come home to Jesus.

Saturday, March 25.

The Lord has been prompting me to get with Albert, whom I prayed with in February to receive Jesus. His life of worldliness hasn't changed. He hasn't plugged into Bellwood church or shown any interest in the Lord.

We sat down at a table together. "Albert, do you remember that wonderful day when we knelt and you invited Jesus to come in and take over your life?"

"Yes."

"When you prayed with me, Albert, did you mean what you said or were you just saying it to please me?"

"Oh, it was real," he asserted.

"Then I'm puzzled, Albert. I see others who have made the same decision become active in the Bible study, but you haven't. They seem hungry to grow and go on with God."

"Well, I still read the Bible on my own." This seemed to show me where he was at. A heart of desire was missing.

"Albert, are you happy with the way you're living your life?"

"No," he confessed.

I drew two circles with a throne in each, with him on one throne and Christ on the other. "Albert, which circle best represents your life?"

He listened and prayed a recommitment prayer. I could only turn him over to the Lord. I don't have a good feeling about our talk. I feel disappointed and helpless. I am sad for him. But, as I sometimes do in counseling, I wrote him out a prescription: Matthew 13:3-9, 18-23 and John 3:36.

Mary visited this morning. I checked for that high beam smile and confident, peaceful air. It came with her. We talked briefly about household finances. She brought greetings and comments from friends at church. We discussed how my being in jail is not merely something to be endured, but an adventure. We are growing and learning from this. We closed in prayer over the phones, separated by the thick glass. Then the guard unlocked the door of the visitation booth to indicate that the visit was over.

I'm a person who files everything from notes to jokes. Envelopes that brought mail now serve as file folders for Mary's letters, other special correspondence, legal papers, pro-life papers, teaching materials, writing materials, and this journal. When I put all of this plus song sheets, Bibles, and New Testaments under my mattress, it can be lumpy.

I'm really enjoying the special Easter music this week on a local Christian station. Having access to daily Christian music means a great deal in jail. It lifts the spirit so wonderfully.

I prayed with a south Georgia fellow to receive Jesus today. He seems sorta slow of thought. *"Let it sink in deep and stick, Lord."*

Another south Georgia boy now in the next bunk consistently calls me "preacher man." When I remarked about this, he said, "That's what we call'um where I live."

Some of the speech is really interesting here. I wonder if a phrase is peculiar to Georgia or the inner-city subculture. A fellow asked another, "Would you like to trade the meat patty for the cobbler?" The answer came: "That'll work." And to say that someone has an "attitude," means they have a bad attitude.

Easter Sunday, March 26.

Christ is risen! At our 7:45 a.m. Easter service we sang, "He Lives," "Christ the Lord is Risen Today," and closed with "My Jesus I love Thee."

Although Mark usually speaks in the morning, I taught today, speaking on Matthew 28:1-9. I emphasized that the rest of the Bible would be meaningless without verse six, "He is not here: for He is risen," and that our responses should be:

(1) "Go quickly and tell. . . that he is risen from the dead" (vs. 7).

(2) Live with great joy (vs. 8).

(3) Worship Jesus daily by service and godly living (vs. 9).

Two newcomers, Harold and Roger, showed up for the Easter service. One fellow raised his hand to get right with Jesus during the altar call.

Most voluntarily shake my hand after each Bible study. I feel like a father with loving children. Brother Mark probably feels similarly toward them.

I appreciate Mark. It's such a blessing to have a brother to discuss various church moves and options with. We both sense the church is something we are doing together. Dividing the responsibility makes it more enjoyable.

Mark can relate to the inner Atlanta world from which most of these fellows come. I cannot. I'm from a small town and suburbia. Mark knows the men and their mind set better than I do. We're a team. I need him. His role is invaluable.

Mark is faithful, always in the group with his deep speaking voice, always there as we lead the Bible study together.

He's the inmate representative for Bellwood Barracks. He represents all of us in periodic meetings with the sheriff and other officers. He is also the TV coordinator, helping to reduce arguments and fights over what to watch.(We're just one, big, happy family here.) Mark has the respect of the men. When he calls the barracks together for a meeting the men respond and listen as when an officer speaks. Mark's a quiet, low key person, but in these meetings his leadership and authority is evident.

It would be a big blow to see Mark go. *"You wouldn't do that to me, would You, Lord?"*

My throat continues to need prayer. My normal teaching voice is not sufficient for the Bible study. With the TV turned up full blast, I must actually shout just to be heard by those seven to eight feet away. It hurts now to talk since the morning service. *"Lord, direct me regarding the evening service and communion. Heal me by Your power."*

While I was sitting at this table writing, the "slow" fellow from rural Georgia just walked up and sat down. He told me he had read Billy Graham's "Steps to Peace with God" which I gave him yesterday. He seems so hungry to learn. Now he's reading aloud from a Scripture leaflet I just gave him. He stumbled on the word "iniquity." Don't we all.

Mark and I got to go to the Chaplain's service this afternoon. Good hymns and a stirring, soul-winning message. This Easter is a warm, sunny, gorgeous day outside. God is a God of beauty and it's planned beauty. Not accidental or occasional, but planned.

We served communion in tonight's Bible study, using orange juice, styrofoam cups, and sliced bread held over from meal time. We pulled up a table in front of our bunks as usual. The brothers watched silently as I stood and broke the bread. They were unusually quiet and attentive as I repeated the powerful, time-honored words: "This is Christ's body broken for you." And then as I poured the orange juice into the cups: "This is Christ's blood shed for you." The believers partook. We paused to reflect on the Savior's pain in dying so that we might avoid eternal suffering.

We have not done any baptizing here. The showers would be the only available means. But we aren't allowed to socialize in the bath area. I'm not under conviction to pursue baptisms. We're seeing conversions. Discipling is going well. Besides, it might be good for them to confirm their new faith out on the street before receiving baptism. I have encouraged them to be baptized after release and to join a good church. This is an artificial situation where the environment keeps them from sin.

Chapter 13

"How Much Longer, Lord?"

Tuesday, March 28.

I've been fasting for two days. I'm wanting to remove any poisons from my system. Mark is a health food buff and suggested it.

More wisdom was delivered directly to my bunk again. Guy Dowd said it on a Christian radio program: "The opposite of love isn't hate, but apathy."

Buddy visited me today. He tried to recall the tune to a praise chorus, "The King of Glory," which I had asked about. I wanted to learn it and teach the others. This was a favorite of mine years ago at summer camp. Now Buddy was helping me to remember. As he shared what he recalled, I chimed in weakly. Our musical rendition wouldn't threaten Handel or Bach, but he gave me a taste for this wonderful song which I had been wanting to rediscover for years.

Last night I spoke to my attorneys, Devin and Matt, on the phone. The papers are awaiting my approval to apply for release through the Pardons and Parole board. *"Lord, do I say 'yes'? Is man saying 'leave,' but God saying 'not yet'? I'll just wait awhile. Jesus, speak in big letters for this skillet-headed Tennessee boy."*

One day while I was in the exercise yard of the Fulton County Jail I got to talking with a resident from another cell block about the sanctity of life. He asked, "Explain to me how breaking the law (to save unborn lives) can be justified?"

I answered, "Do you agree with the peaceful, civil disobedience that Martin Luther King, Jr. and others participated in? Should they have done that?"

He said thoughtfully, "I see what you mean."

Wednesday, March 29.

A letter from my precious wife:

Dearest Husband:

Read Psalm 91 again this a.m. That has been the psalm I run to when in need. Was reminded

of a thought from verse 14 about knowing His
name: "Because He has set His love upon me,
therefore will I deliver him: I will set him on
high, because he has known My name." A cross
reference reminded me that Paul's suffering was
for the sake of the Gospel. What I currently
don't know of His name I pray I will learn over
these weeks."

All My Love,

Mary

Another letter that touched me came from a young girl:

Dear Mr. Fred:

I know what your doing is right. I would be
down in Georgia with you except I'm only 11.

Abortion is wrong! and what your doing I think
makes God awfully proud!

Friday, March 31.

Our budding Bible study leader, Carl, went to court today. He is
to be released within hours. He's delighted. I hate to see Carl go.
He is a vital, joyful cog in our church. I'll miss his smiling face and
youthful exuberance.

I made these points to the attentive group on soul winning
tonight:

(1) Boldness overcomes fear and creates opportunities for witnessing. Pray for boldness.

(2) Recover the urgency. Witnessing should be high priority for
the individual and the church.

(3) Expect some criticism from within and beyond the church.
Jesus and the disciples had opposition.

(4) Be a professional. A good doctor doesn't stop after identifying
the problem. He assumes the patient wants it fixed. Unsaved
sinners urgently need heart surgery. Finish the job.

I noted that Luke 15:7, 10 offers a unique glimpse inside the
window of heaven. "... Joy shall be in heaven over one sinner that
repents ... There is joy in the presence of the angels... "

I told them: "First, we can actually influence praise meetings in
heaven. Second, angels are concerned about repentance and souls
being saved. Third, praise, repentance, and souls being saved are
linked together. Rejoicing and soul winning are companions, not

competitors. Fourth, heaven isn't ho-hum or bashful when one gets saved. Heavenly maturity doesn't outgrow soul winning."

Saturday, April 1.

I was surprised to hear Mark say that I should get out of jail. I wonder about his reason. Is he just thinking of me, or Mary, rather than the church here? I don't feel led to remain here indefinitely for the church's sake. Yet, I don't want to chicken out either. *"Lord, speak powerfully. Oh Jesus, there are so many lost lambs here."*

Unfortunately Albert, the fellow I had the recommitment talk and prayer with the other day, has still not been to the group or noticeably altered his secular behavior. This is truly disappointing for one who says he received Jesus. The Lord will have to handle his case from here. He hasn't hit bottom yet.

Church friends on the outside keep sending us books. Twelve or fifteen arrived yesterday. I've wondered how to make the most of our books? I decided to spread them out on my bunk and let passersby check them out. So far, six "library books" have been taken today, plus two or three of the Christian magazines Mary sent me.

"Pack it up" is a wonderful, long awaited word in this place. It normally means you are ready for release. One joker woke up a man saying, "Pack it up." He had him scrambling around, throwing his stuff together, preparing to leave.

The locked door hasn't kept out the April Fool jokes. One was pulled by Brother Mark, our inmate representative, though one had to be here to appreciate it. Mark called out the names of men he said were going to court (often a long awaited, desirable event), but really were not. How crestfallen they were when Mark called out, "April fool!" Another joker told a deputy that the rear door was unlocked. Such is jailhouse humor.

Sunday, April 2.

It's 11:25 a.m. and pastors are proclaiming the Bible all over Atlanta. Pastors need courage to teach specifically on family prayer time, parental discipline, tithing, divorce, remarriage, killing of the unborn, removal of church members living in gross sin, and other needs. Churches need to back up their pastors with appropriate policies where Scripturally applicable. Pastors need the prayers of the faithful. Proclaiming all of God's truth is a tough job at best. Yet weak pulpits produce weak Christians.

More than any other chapter in the Bible, we keep returning here to Psalm 119. I want to use our valuable Bible study time to impart a deep appreciation of God's Word. In simple ways, I keep re-emphasizing that the Bible is God breathed, inspired, inerrant, authoritative, and totally reliable.

Accepting the whole Bible as true isn't what bothers many people. It's carrying out individual verses. For all of us it's easier to accept the authority of the Word in theory than to "walk" it out (Romans 7:19). The problem may not be categorically denying the authority of the Bible, but just ignoring verses that offend. Opting for a more "humane," "loving," approach over taking the Bible "legally" or "literally" can be a blind spot. Am I more loving than God Himself? Should I try to veto the Lord's eternal wisdom?

Our will to obey God is inadequate. Since Adam, our minds, wills, and emotions have all been sinfully corrupted. They are not functioning as they could. Our old nature rebels against authority, including commands in Holy Scripture.

Monday, April 3.

This is the closing from Mary's latest letter:

> . . . The challenge to me today was from Isaiah 2:22: "Stop trusting in man" (NIV). . . . The Lord will help us in this, Honey. I love you and want you home, but far more [I] want you where you are needed for Him.
>
> All My Love,
>
> Mary

In a lighter moment I inwardly laughed. How will I ever get out of here with a wife talking and praying as she does? But I treasure her faithful letters and words.

I'm advising my attorneys that I don't want to pursue the Pardons and Parole Board application at this time. It's hard to say why. It might be a quick out, but I just don't have the peace about it that I do about the State Appeals Court option.

God will deliver us from dead ends, delays, and unknown snares if we will just listen to Him. In such situations as mine, this seems doubly important. Feelings run high on abortion. You don't always get a fair shake. In this judicial mine field I want to hear from God and lean on Him more than my logic alone. Logic said that David, the little shepherd boy, didn't stand a chance against the big, experienced, well-armed Goliath. God can guide so marvelously, if we will listen.

For example, I was two to three haircuts behind and looking for the emergency entrance to the barber shop. The regular trustee that cuts hair disappeared before he got to me. I worked on my hair a bit with my razor rather ineptly. Then among the 59 other men in our unit I was prompted to ask one particular fellow if he could help.

"Yes," he promptly replied. "That's what I do on the street. I cut hair."

I got a better haircut than I probably would have received from the trustee. *"Thank You, Jesus."*

Listening to the Spirit of God has its little fringe benefits. In other situations one's life could depend on it. God may use the small, trivial incidents to teach us to listen well so when the biggies come along we'll be all ears. Often "hearing from God" simply means having peace about something before we act. I need continual practice in hearing that still small voice.

I'm reading C. S. Lewis' **The Screwtape Letters**, just received from friends in my home church. Praise God for their faithful love. I was reading the chapter on gluttony. This vice is presented as not only overeating but being picky about what is served. It could be craving pizza so much that we won't eat the tuna fish. Does gluttony encompass unthankfulness?

Tuesday, April 4.

I went out with some guys for an hour's worth of morning exercise in the yard. I walk or jog, although volleyball, basketball, football, and exercise bars are also available. Rain hit as soon as we got outside so we came right back in. I did some indoor exercising and hit the shower.

Male and female officers are used interchangeably here. Only a chain link fence and a shoulder high barrier separates the officers' station from the totally open bathroom area. Their station is floor level except for a four-foot high, raised platform enclosed by a second fence. It's like a cage within a cage. The supervising sergeant sits in the perch and controls the door, fan, and light switches. He or she has better visibility than the two deputies down on the floor.

Male or female officers on the upper level platform can see somewhat more of the bath area if they choose to. Modesty in the showers calls for a bit of adaptability. A few of us simply wear shorts while showering.

Today the shower was possessed by three evil speaking fellows when I arrived. They are from the adjoining 1B2 area we share the bath with.

"Lord, what is my best approach?"

I did what one often does in showers—sing! I began with the gentle, "Oh, How I Love Jesus," then moved into second gear with "Power in the Blood." The immoral conversation immediately wilted and died. Showers are for cleansing. I wish all the filthy talk here could be stopped as easily. Maybe we should sing more hymns on the job, at bowling alleys, school, or home.

Thursday, April 6.

Surrounded with so much filthy language and heaviness here, I find praise to be a refreshing change. Praise sparks enthusiasm. Praise emboldens. It gets our thoughts off self. It switches us over to God's frequency when we're struggling with the blahs, or faith-hindering thoughts.

Full bodied praise breaks inhibitions. It may expose latent pride. At times I find myself not wanting to really let go and praise Him with a whole heart.

"Praise You, Lord of Lords and King of Kings! Fill me with Your Spirit this morning. I must have it."

The flesh often resists early morning praise, as it does other forms of prayers. "The spirit is willing, but the flesh is weak (Matthew 26:41). When I don't feel like arising in the early morning and praising Him with song and voice, that is probably when I need it most. Praise is commanded. Praise is an act of the will, not feelings. Feelings may or may not follow later.

Besides a theology of sin, I want to carry out a theology of praise. Praise is like an elevator, taking us above ourselves and our little world. It's switching over to God's frequency when we're in a blah mood. It takes our eyes off of self.

Full bodied praise even exposes pride and rebellion. We often put up resistance to letting go, even when we're praising God with the same vigor as we cheer at a ball game.

Being here I miss the freedom to be totally alone and sing early morning hymns and songs to Jesus. I miss the meditation and vocal freedom that being surrounded by 59 other people denies. But God is faithful in our circumstances.

Cool today and no heat. This concrete building can be damp. I've got on flannel pajama tops, two T-shirts, and two long john tops.

Who doesn't like to be called for meal time? Yet to be awakened for breakfast or supper with an officer's yell, "Trays are up!" somehow lacks the warmth and aesthetic charm of home cooking and family closeness. That's the "dinner bell" for us, though.

In defense of the officers, it should be said that some inmates would probably not otherwise get out of bed on time for meals. They'd complain 15 minutes later, "Nobody woke me up. Now I'm not going to get any food 'till breakfast tomorrow. Give me a complaint form."

If I were an officer, I might use a train whistle. I'm gaining more and more insight into how certain rules and procedures evolved for inmates. It's a lot like the army.

So many here could surely have avoided jail, if they'd had a good father figure and/or Jesus sitting on the throne of their lives. Instead they double-parked outside Hell's ticket office. It's such a waste. It's tragic.

Therefore, no theology will work that sweeps hard-heartedness and sin under the rug. Such theology will do no more good than trying to sweeten up a wild boar with maple syrup.

Time and again a non-church member or jail officer will inquire, "When are you leaving? Isn't it about time for you to be getting out?" More than once I've replied with a very gentle, "Somebody's got to lead people to Jesus." And with some I smilingly add a gospel seed, "Are you gonna do that?" They seem to understand and give a nodding approval to my answer.

Most of those praying to receive the Lord are more on the young side than middle-aged or older. Many are under 25 or 30. A few older fellows have jumped on board, though. I can think of two older fellows whose decisions are proving to be valid. Perhaps they don't play games as much as the younger ones, unless they're just off the street or trying to impress to get something from you.

I had a quick, evangelistic conversation with a young fellow yesterday. Kent had been a 250 lb. running back on a college team and could do the 40-yard dash in 4.6. In passing, I inquired, "Are you interested in spiritual things?. . . Which way would you go if you died tonight? . . . Have you been born again?" It's easy to prompt thinking about eternal issues. Questions with power can jump start spiritual thinking. Kent said he was not saved. Who should show up at Bible study last night but Kent! He and another fellow, Harry, responded to the altar call.

Another new man I had questioned earlier looked me up about 11:30 last night. We talked. He prayed to receive the Lord around midnight and I gave him my normal follow-up teaching, complete with new believers' pamphlet.

I never tell a fellow that he's saved, though. I prefer that he convince me with his words and changed behavior. That's especially true here where we see some follow through while others prove to have "rocky soil" hearts.

I grieve for those who don't change or evidence any long term fruit befitting repentance. I feel so helpless . . . , so helpless. I at least have a minuscule glimpse of what our Lord must have felt when weeping over rebellious Jerusalem (Matthew 23:37). There is one thing even an all powerful God can't do anything about, a sinner's unyielding rebellion (Isaiah 5:4). But resistant soil is not to deter us from further sowing.

There just isn't enough of me or hours in the day to build in-depth, ongoing friendships with 59 men, or even half of them. Group evangelism, literature, and initial contact witnessing are needful means if many are to be reached.

Mary's preacher dad, Francis Neddo, came to visit me today. It was good to see his beaming face and peaceful countenance. He's in town for a pastors' seminar. He told me about his recent trip to Israel. His coming was an answer to prayer. I needed to see his smiling face. We enjoyed warm fellowship and ended bowing before the throne of grace together.

As usual, an officer walked with me back to Bellwood. He told me he was saved. He said, "I stopped by and listened in on your Bible study last night. I knew then that you weren't here on 'charges,' but on a mission."

Another letter from Mary. She closed,

```
You are very much in my prayers, Sweetie. I
sense this is a time of trust for both of us.
It is becoming sweet for me and I trust for you
also. Fellowship with Him is more precious and
finally, I believe I'm learning to walk out the
Word . . . and let the Word dwell in me throughout
```

the day. That has not been a strong charac-
teristic for me over the years.

   I love you, Sweetie.

   Mary

This experience is drawing Mary and me closer together. It's adding a sense of purpose and mission. There's joy in being on the cutting edge of something vital.

Chapter 14

"The 'Open Letter' to Officials"

Saturday, April 8.

Rainy and cool outside. Our ceiling and walls bead up and drip moisture. Even though it's humid and damp, a few residents complain if the fresh air fan is turned on. They begin shouting, so the sergeant in charge often just turns the fan off. But on warm days most sergeants let it run for hours. That's wonderful.

Many are wearing blankets today. I have on a long john top, with my pajama top folded in half and tied around my head giving a Middle Eastern look.

Attorney Matt Coles really encouraged me during his visit today. I shared with him my idea of writing an open letter to officials that would clarify two matters: (1) My position on paying the fine, and (2) Why I'm still here and not out on appeal bond as Brenda Roberts is. Matt concurred with the idea.

We sent this letter to key officials, legislators, and media.

Gentlemen:

I am a Southern Baptist minister who was convicted with Brenda Roberts on January 31, 1989 only for protecting human life. For this first-time misdemeanor, I received four one-year sentences, with all but 30 days suspended on the condition that I pay a $1,760 fine.

It might be helpful for me to clarify my position on two matters:

First, due to the unusual sentences received, Brenda Roberts and I are now appealing our case. Speaking for myself, if the Appeals Court directs me to pay any or all of the $1,760 fine, I will fully and promptly comply. Win or lose we will have had our day in court.

The criminal justice system is not our enemy. The system should be commended, as it dispenses justice with integrity and even-handedness. Any blame basically is ours due to our 16-year tardiness in responding to the silent cries of unborn babies.

Second, why am I still in jail six weeks after my 30-day sentence has been completed? I understand that I can leave any time by paying an appeal bond of $1,760.

By being here, I have hopefully been able to identify in a small way with the ultimate penalty, death, received by unborn babies every day.

Also, while here in jail the Lord has graciously opened doors to a ministry among fellow inmates. My heart is touched by the lostness and broken lives of many here. New friends are hurting and bleeding from the wounds of sin. Most are here on alcohol or drug-related charges.

Having such a wonderful Lord caring for me, the least I can do is minister to others in need while in here. It has pleased my precious Lord to delay my departure for His own purposes. Jesus cares about the poor, born or unborn, and the needy. Should we do less?

Cordially,

Bro. Fred F. Kerr

Inmate No. 406417

Fulton County Jail

Chapter 15

"Of Testimonies and Tracts"

Tuesday, April 11.

Being around so much filthy language and aimless living can simplify one's theology. Twice daily here each man can arise, walk one way and hear God's Word taught, or walk the other way and run from Jesus. Bellwood is a vignette of the scene people have acted out daily through the centuries. Will a person choose for or against God today? TV or truth? Worldliness or worship? Judgment or Jesus?

Sin traps. Sin has much stronger bars than this jail. Iron rusts over time. Sin becomes stronger and thirstier.

I heard that **The Atlanta Journal and Constitution** wants to interview me if they can obtain permission from the Sheriff's office. I was also told that CBN television wanted to come in with a camera man and talk to me, but was denied permission. But praise the Lord! He's in control. I'm on the winning side.

Wednesday, April 12:

John and Swifty are two of our newest Bellwood residents. One is here for non-support. The other has a drinking problem. Both sought me out.

John, who is from south Georgia, said I looked like a preacher. He wins you over with his down home, sincere manner. He initially asked for something to read. I gave him my two favorite tracts. Mary will send me more as I run low. Both have excellent salvation themes with many power verses.

John and Swifty both prayed to receive Jesus yesterday and gave their salvation testimonies in the group this morning. *"Thank You, Jesus. Hold them close."*

After they pray to receive Jesus, I ask our new converts to go and tell someone of their big decision right away. I often go along with them for support. Going public helps settle the matter way down deep. It's like a couple running their engagement picture in the

paper. I also ask each new convert to give his testimony in the Bible
study. "For God hath not given us the spirit of fear, but of power,
and of love, and of a sound mind. Be not thou therefore ashamed
of the testimony of our Lord . . " (1 Tim. 1:7-8a).

A public salvation testimony serves several purposes:

(1) It helps the new convert conceptualize and verbalize his new
faith and increases his confidence and boldness. If one doesn't push
on into bold witnessing, the danger is that you can become just a
frustrated, armchair evangelist. New Testament evangelists
weren't embarrassed to boldly proclaim the gospel to all who would
listen.

(2) One's testimony edifies and encourages the saints as they see
real fruit from witnessing efforts.

(3) It helps others get to know a new believer, befriend him, and
meet his needs. The new Christian becomes integrated into the
church family: "Welcome, Bill. I heard you say you are from
Augusta. Well, so am I. Can you have lunch with us today?"

(4) Above all, a testimony at any time glorifies God who gives the
increase.

We need more wet-eyed testimonies and less fast food religion.

I had a deliverance prayer with Swifty. He wants to enter a detox
center to get loose from liquor.

Swifty strikes me as an easy-going street person. He's small and
appears not to be very disciplined in his mind. He appears to be
quickly influenced by what those around him say. He needs Jesus
and backbone. Addiction drains godly resistance from the will.

In addition to alcohol, it's sad to see so many here who are totally
hooked on tobacco. Most guys roll their own cigarettes because it's
cheaper. Some trade their food for cigarettes. Others are addicted
to games of chance. They'll gamble away their own dinner. No
wonder money is not allowed in the barracks.

Bellwood guys are like people everywhere. A TV, a little carpet
on the floor, and a six-pack to suck on is about all the heaven they
seem interested in. Flesh and faith can't co-exist. We can't walk
deeply in the Spirit and the flesh. They are like fire and water. One
will overpower and dominate the other.

It's nine o'clock and the evening Bible study is over. Mark taught
on repentance. The rising release rate has pushed our attendance
down to about six.

The judges and courts are really turning the inmates loose right now. A Federal court order to reduce overcrowding in the Fulton County Jail is evidently impacting sentencing. I'm hearing that fines are being levied or increased in lieu of giving inmates more jail time.

Of the reported 2,100 prisoners here in a facility built for 900, over 1900 are in the two-story, brick building beside our barracks. No wonder the courts have ordered the population be reduced. Being here and seeing firsthand the very high turnover rate in these limited facilities I now have some feel for just how many more violators there are out there than there is jail space for them. It's not a good situation.

Officers remind the unruly among us that Bellwood is preferable to other cell blocks. Many of our people are first time offenders, as I am. They're mostly non-violent types. The staff here generally seems to be making the best of a tough situation.

Occasionally someone will start a fire or try to escape, as happened recently in the exercise yard. The yard is enclosed by two 15- to 20-foot high fences topped by rolled barbed wire, with guards on every side. Recently four or five inmates from the main building wrapped towels around their arms and bodies and simply climbed the fence. For some reason the guard who was supposed to be at that end of the yard was not there. A vehicle or cycle was waiting. Two got away. The others did not. I wasn't out there that day, but the guys came back in buzzing about what they had witnessed.

My heart went out to a church member today who's been separated from his wife for 11 years. He's been living in sin with a girl he cares for very much and would like to marry. If he files for divorce he could be hit with thousands of dollars in unpaid support and jail time. He asked me what to do.

Principle: Sin is like engine trouble, the longer it is ignored, the higher your repair bill.

Friday, April 14.

George and Jack went to court today. Both are to be released. George came in with me on January 31st.

I gave Jack more tracts to take with him. He said he gave out some, along with his testimony, while awaiting trial today.

It was a black day when the Devil convinced many Christians that distributing tracts was lowly, unsophisticated, and unworthy of a mature believer's time. To use such literature in evangelism is to be on the side of giants in the faith from the early church

fathers to John Calvin, Martin Luther, John Wesley, George
Whitefield, and Dwight L. Moody. Tracts are patient, waiting for
months and years to be read. They don't get into arguments. They
are effective and fruitful.

Being here gives time to review priorities and reflect on the chaff
and wheat in one's life and in Christianity. Riches and entertainment bid for our time. American Christianity is producing many
who want the riches of Solomon, but precious few who desire the
life of the prophet Elijah. The majority prefer the palace's play toys
over the prophet's power. More and more I'm seeing that I can't
have both. If I spend more than a certain amount of time with play
toys the zeal and freshness seems to start diminishing. I suspect
there is an invisible line for each believer. If we cross over into
excessive recreation or other activities, closeness with Jesus and
anointing spring a leak. Numbness overtakes zeal.

The old nature says, "You can have both." But our zeal soon
departs. We want abnormal power, but a "normal" life. Will God
hook up a 500-horsepower tractor to a one-mule plow?

I'm not against entertainment. The point is that a price must be
paid to gain more from God. God and the electric company agree:
power costs. Do I want thirty, sixty, or hundred-fold fruit?

The answer isn't legalism. Legalism can be self-deceiving. Nor
is the answer scorn for serious, daily prayer and Bible time. Some
think a legalist is any believer who has more discipline than they
have.

The answer is found in quality time with Jesus. It's hungering
after Him. I must have that daily filling with the Holy Spirit.

Salvation is free but power with God is expensive. Whether in
the natural or spiritual realm, prime roast beef costs more than
hamburger. It is one thing to read the price tag and quite another
to pay it.

*"Lord, I confess that time and again I see the advantage of the
'prime roast,' yet my busyness buys only 'burgers.' Continue to
increase my desire to spend time with You."*

Mary comes tonight. She can come on a Friday and see me on
both Saturday and Sunday sometimes. I'm looking forward to her
visits.

She's bringing a fresh supply of T-shirts and white socks. Mine
have grown dingy over the weeks. We have no access to a laundry,
though we can turn in our blue uniforms to be washed. The system
has holes, though. Some inmates put their name on the laundry
list to receive back a uniform when they haven't turned one in. I

lost my extra pair of pants that way. Later a nice sergeant got me a replacement.

George came to see me after returning from court and to say that he would be leaving. He was here for four to six weeks before attending our Bible study. He responded to the altar call on Easter Sunday. His was no "Release-me-quick, Lord" prayer. I doubt that he has missed two of our twice-daily meetings since he asked Jesus into his heart.

In his final meeting with our church I inquired, "Brother George, is there anything you would like to say before you leave us?"

"Yes," he testified to our group. "Brother Kerr and I came in together. I was hostile. I would probably be locked up now for fighting if I hadn't been saved. Now I'm a new man. I don't need the old ways any more. Praise God, I'm leaving different than I came.

"My mother prayed for me for years. I called her long distance to tell her, 'Momma, I got saved.' She was so happy."

George's fine testimony encouraged us all.

Chapter 16

"Rolling Dice, Reporters, and Root Spells"

Monday, April 17.

I'm still awaiting response from the open letter attorney Matt Coles and I sent to officials and media. I'm impressed from studying Philippians recently to follow Christ's example in relating to the criminal justice system. Jesus was a suffering servant. He was unjustly tried and sentenced. Yet He remained humble and was not belligerent or defiant toward authorities.

Christ did not let the world's authorities compromise His heaven-ordained agenda. He was humble when arrested, put on trial, and during sentencing. But He didn't change His game plan. He didn't back down on His commitment. He maintained a right attitude and gentle spirit.

About 12:20 this morning I asked two teenagers if they would quiet down as people around them were trying to sleep. They had been shooting dice with excessive noise and abandon. They ignored my request and switched to loudly tapping out rap music and singing. Within an hour they got into an argument and a bathroom fight with an equally demonstrative Cuban they had awakened. The jail officers immediately transferred the rappers to another, no doubt, less desirable unit.

They hadn't acted quite this out-of-control before. Satan was prodding.

I sensed a deliberate intentional loudness with a devil-may-care attitude. Not surprisingly, the rappers had resisted the Gospel from us for weeks. How sad. At times the soul winner wants to do more than he is able to with the resistant. But then it's a comfort to remember that I can't save souls in any case, only God's Spirit can bring them to the Savior.

Tuesday, April 18.

I did an interview with Lorri Denise Booker of **The Atlanta Journal and Constitution** this afternoon. She was the same reporter who interviewed us during the trial, except today she brought a photographer in with her. We talked in a contact visitation booth where only the wire mesh separated us, not glass. She seemed to be wanting a human interest, behind the scenes, home life kind of story. I suggested that she "focus on the issues, not me." The article is to run Thursday morning.

Seven attended our evening Bible study on Isaac and Rebekah, Part Two. Two new fellows who prayed to receive the Lord last night returned and a new arrival came also. Word came that W.D., an alumnus of our Bellwood church, has had a car accident. We prayed for him and passed around a get well note for everyone to sign.

Wearing crosses around the neck have suddenly become popular here among non-church men. Is this some kind of secularist, counterfeit revival? Is it a counter attack on the real thing? The crosses are made by rolling up the tin foil that loose tobacco comes in and wrapping the foil with red thread. I was even offered a free cross. Others buy them, I presume.

Two spiritually adrift fellows drew me aside after Bible study and asked if I would bless their crosses to aid in warding off root spells. I explained that I "didn't know of any Bible verses that encourage that. The Holy Spirit's power enters people, not objects. He fills and ministers through His people, not material things. Our bodies are the temple or residence of the Holy Spirit. His power is available to us through prayer as the Holy Spirit empowers."

They shrugged and walked away. These two fellows wanted God's protection and power, but not enough to get right with Jesus and plug into the Bible study. I suspect they have been influenced by an occult-oriented series that has been on TV this week. Everyone wants a little dab of religion. Power is popular, righteousness isn't. "God is a Spirit: and they that worship Him must worship Him in spirit and in truth" (John 4:24).

Wednesday, April 19.

I'm still praying and hoping that tomorrow's newspaper article will be for Jesus' purposes. I don't want it focused on me, but rather on the reason I'm here. *"Move, Lord Jesus!"*

I did my daily walking around the room today while quietly singing rich hymns of the faith. "Jesus Shall Reign" and the praise chorus, "In Moments Like These" are my particular favorites at this time.

This afternoon I'm thinking how I can best impart to young believers the duty and joy awaiting them if they turn loose of their side of the pool and step into the deep water on faith. Much of what passes for depression, I believe, is nothing more than bored Christians unwilling to push out and take risks in ministry. Too many of us are over-taught and under-fought. Much joy and excitement is waiting.

What perpetually gloomy believers often need is not more dusty seminar notebooks, or another drawer of cassette tapes. Let's take a scary leap of faith into vital ministry and servanthood. Super fulfillment is waiting where big and hurting needs are.

Thursday, April 20.

Inmate trustees work in the commissary, food service, laundry and in various other work areas. They receive two days off their sentence for every one day served. They also get some small privileges like coats in cold winter, a little money, and more freedom of movement. Some fellows get restless being cooped up in Bellwood and apply to be a trustee just for a change.

I could be a trustee, but it would negate the reason I'm here which is to minister in Bellwood. This is a full time job for me. Out of curiosity I did inquire about serving as a chaplain's aide of some sort, but got no reply.

My newspaper—which I pay for—was delivered early this morning as usual. A friendly trustee brings it right up to the door in the chain link fence that separates us from the officers' station. I often greet him with a lusty "Praise the Lord." He is a short, graying man with glasses and lots of talk. He handed me the receipt sheet through the gate to sign and said, "Hey, being a trustee is not so bad. You ought to put your name in." He doesn't know about my ministry with the Bellwood church.

Because it was time for the Bible study, I put the paper aside for later reading. Before I could read it, an officer brought me a second copy of the front page on which was Lori Booker's article.

The story, titled "Abortion Protester Calls Jail God's Will," came complete with a picture of me in living color. Overall, the coverage was positive with only a couple of inaccuracies. The writer gave the facts of my case and noted that I could get out by posting a $1,760 appeal bond or pay the $1,760 fine, but that I would not feel at peace if I did leave. She quoted me correctly as saying that I am only "ready to leave when God gives me the green light. I'm here to identify with the penalty the unborn pay. We don't blame the judicial system. It's ultimately our fault for having waited 16 years to respond to the crimes committed against these unborn babies. We're not trying to pick a fight with anyone."

The writer quoted Michael Hirsh, director of Operation Rescue/Atlanta, as saying that I might be the first of many who decide their principles are more important than their freedom. "This just shows the commitment of the people who want to see the end of legalized child-killing in Atlanta," he continued. "We're willing to give up our rights for somebody we don't even know."

The article also included a testimony by phone from Mary: "I'm very much behind [Fred] because I am desirous of seeing that unborn babies are saved. I appreciate the courage and boldness he has to live out his convictions in this way."

As I think about this newspaper testimony going out all over Atlanta and beyond, I pray, *"Use it, Lord, for Your purposes. Touch the hearts of real believers, to reach out in compassion and seek justice for the helpless innocents."*

In tonight's Bible study, I taught on Christ vs. Satan and our spiritual weapons in this warfare. The guys seemed gripped by this subject. I spoke far longer than usual, about an hour.

We need to remember that the Devil is not omnipresent. Neither he nor his evil spirits can be everywhere at once. And Satan has only a finite number of fallen angels, or demonic spirits. They are already outnumbered two to one by good angels. Therefore the more people he can kill the higher proportion of those still living he can deploy demonic spirits to attack. Obviously the more that can be killed quickly the less outnumbered his forces will be and the more influence he will have.

Chapter 17

"Pro-Life: The New Missions Frontier for the Church"

Sunday, April 23.

Today I was escorted back from visitation by a fine sergeant who happened not to have handcuffs to put on me. I immediately placed my hands behind my back in handcuff position and said, "Well, I guess I'll just have to pretend." We enjoyed a congenial conversation walking back.

After some weeks here, some experimentation, and wondering how much to share the Gospel with officers, I've learned that this 150-yard walk to visitation and back is a good witnessing opportunity. Most are open to talking. Many are curious as to what I'm doing here, or why I haven't gotten out yet.

I experienced a touch of community in the barracks today. I don't watch TV here, except for some news and odds and ends, but I did cast a losing vote for the baseball game last night. A middle-aged, non-church member came to me afterwards and testily vowed, "You will get to watch your game tomorrow, I promise you!" I guess he figured that as little as I watch, I ought to have a say so once in a while.

Somehow it came to pass today and the game was not vetoed. He came to get me at my bunk when the game came on. Though I watch TV least of all on Sundays, I didn't have the heart not to honor his efforts for awhile.

A pro-lifer, who visited me today, lamented, "I can't seem to get my church concerned about abortion."

Apathy abounds. Yet it is difficult to get Christians to call it by name. Too few believers are involved in the political fight against abortion, pornography, drugs, and other evils. Being out front can be lonely. The high road is not well traveled. Traffic jams shouldn't be expected there.

The church has now been retreating from the cities for three decades. Flight continues, even though problems like drugs and crime have followed us to the suburbs. Soon we will have to stand and fight or be totally overrun. God seems to be boxing us in. Still, I suppose that some Christians unfortunately will try to retreat back to a mountain cabin to escape societal problems, but most won't.

Because of so little sanctity of life teaching in most Protestant churches over the past 16 years, a mindset of apathy has built up. I doubt that this will be overcome overnight. Repeated teaching and role models of involvement are needed.

A new pastor can come to a church that is not missions-oriented and his teaching and excitement be so infectious that in two years they will have a fine missions emphasis. So can it be with pro-life missions. *"So let it be, Lord."*

Sanctity of life may just be a new missions frontier, because the issue has yet to gain entrance into missions conferences and magazines. Small, struggling, local, pro-life groups have yet to be considered for most church missions budgets.

God declares in Leviticus 20:3 (NASV) that child sacrifice defiles His sanctuary and profanes His holy name. If that be true, how can the sacrifice of the unborn to convenience not be worthy of consideration for the church missions budget? What stronger words could God have used to consider the killing of innocent children?

Pulling the arms and legs off of precious unborn is still merely an intellectual debate in many church circles. Apathy hides amidst all the verbage today. Except for token appearances at pro-life rallies, support is largely silent. Perhaps it's so traumatic and heavy that our knee-jerk feeling is to avoid it.

Some Christians repeatedly raise the issue, "Is it important to halt abortions until we believers have homes for all the 'unwanted' babies that will be born?" This is sort of like asking, "Why stop a murderer from stabbing his victim unless we know for sure that the emergency room has available space?"

Certainly Christians should reach out in love to all the hurting, needy babies and mothers they can. At the same time we need not let guilt be dumped on us. Sin does carry consequences. One reason premarital or irresponsible intercourse is so evil is that it leaves unmet needs and hurting people—both babies and adults—in its wake.

Pro-lifers want to help. We will continue to help. We can do more. But sinners need not use pro-lifers as a whipping boy or excuse for the consequences of their behavior. Acceptance and repentance of responsibility for their actions is called for as well.

While so many Christians sleep, it's obvious that events in this nation are building toward a moral—or should we say immoral—climax. If we fail to face up to sin, God may have little choice. As happened so frequently in Old Testament Israel and Judah, either purity or purging is on the way for America. God surely cannot continue to allow this slaughter of the innocent to continue unabated.

Thankfully, the Lord is raising up some churches and pastors to report to the trenches. Praise God, it's not nearly as lonely as it was just a short time ago for pro-life workers. There is much untapped potential in the Body of Christ. Energy and funds are there. Only pulpit teaching and role models are needed to unleash them.

Chapter 18

"A Soul Winner is a Surgeon"

If I were a marathon runner this morning, I would be wanting to catch a second wind, or shift into a lower gear. I feel drained. It's times like these when body and emotions waver that the will must see us through.

Our treasure is in earthen vessels. I fight this and don't like to admit I can't do everything endlessly without getting tired or showing any frailty.

"Jesus, forbid that your church here should suffer from my words or witness. It is your bride, a part of your body, and must be found ready for You. Jesus, bring me home to heaven rather than let me hinder You.

"I love You, Jesus. I need You, Lord. I bow before your throne this morning. Praise be to You. Fill me with your precious Holy Spirit today. Empower me. Anoint me for ministry today. Keep me from the Evil One.

"Watch over my precious Mary. Keep her from the Evil One. In Jesus' Name, Amen."

John, a faithful church member, and I are having morning devotions together right now. It's fulfilling to see guys like him really plug into the Word. He's been working on a Bible correspondence lesson also.

John's hunger to grow in the Lord and his gentle spirit make him delightful to be around. Sitting on the adjoining bunk, this south Georgia fellow just confided, "You're the second white man I've ever known whom I can trust." John and I have a real good friendship in the Lord. Since Mary and I don't have any kids, it's good to have spiritual children like John.

"The joy of the Lord is [my] strength" (Nehemiah 8:10). Joy is a daily choice. By choosing to receive "the joy of the Lord" through His Word and prayer we can receive this strength. To choose to junk up the mind with negative and critical data is to vote against strength for the day.

Choosing to be plain and straightforward with the saved and unsaved builds respect and trust. Isn't that what Jesus did with Nicodemus (John 3:3, 7) and with the woman at the well (John 4:16)? A fellow may disagree with the soul winner at the time, but if he knows deep down that he is telling him the truth and doing it in his best interest, he will be respectful.

Evangelists should be professional and follow through. I remember once lying in bed for a couple of days with pain in my abdomen. Neither my parents nor I could figure out what ailed me. They called Dr. Garrison. He came and began poking around and asking doctor questions. Finally he touched where my appendix was located. Touchdown! It hurt, but he had found the source of my trouble. Once convinced of my need, he called for an immediate operation. Feeling that pain, I accepted his diagnosis.

The personal evangelist, if professional in manner, must also find the soul's need and then offer a remedy.

The true spiritual surgeon completes the operation and removes the bullet of sin which has infected the heart of every man. He doesn't leave the patient at death's door. He ministers to the hurting, uncleansed wound. He pours in the healing Balm of Gilead. Jesus is still in the forgiveness business. Bless His precious name!

Doesn't every lost person deserve at least once before he dies, to be brought into the spiritual doctor's office and talked to plainly about his potentially terminal sickness—sin?

The hearse is already on the way to pick up the unsaved sinner. Our only hope is to get there first. We need to rediscover the urgency in reaching the lost. Good surgeons don't dilly dally. Effective soul winners should not either.

I want to press in with the sinner. It takes pursuit because the old sinful nature is experienced at ducking and delaying tactics. An eternal soul is worth it though. Persistence wins. " . . . Behold, now is the accepted time; behold, now is the day of salvation" (2 Corinthians 6:2).

Chapter 19

"The Big Surprise"

Saturday, April 29.

Bellwood is now one fourth empty and more are to leave shortly. The Federal court order to reduce inmate population is in full swing.

The atmosphere here yesterday was like kids on the last day of school. Each man was wondering if he would be among the chosen.

I, too, find myself hoping to be released. Prisoners sentenced for misdemeanors are supposed to get high priority. That's me!

The excitement mounts as each batch of two or three names is called out from hour to hour. Shouts of delight fill the barracks. I smile and am happy for friends as I see their joy, while also knowing that part of my bittersweet experience is leaving with them.

How will they fare on the street? Will they find a good shepherd who really cares for their souls? Can they locate a church where essential Bible doctrines are faithfully taught, like the inspiration and inerrancy of the Word of God, the virgin birth of Jesus, the necessity and efficacy of the substitionary death of our Savior, His bodily resurrection, and second coming?

Sunday, April 30.

Reduction of the inmate population in the Fulton County Jail has become a big news story in the Atlanta area. More are to be released tomorrow. One inmate let out was allegedly picked back up within two hours on an attempted mugging charge.

Our barracks is almost half empty. Ten of the 37 remaining inmates attended tonight's study on God's covenant with Abraham in Genesis 12. Two prayed to turn their lives over to Christ. Another prayed for strength to stay off drugs. Altar calls for attenders to commit themselves to the Lord immediately are as effective as they are Scriptural (Luke 19:9; Acts 2:41, 16:29-34).

I want a break of some sort. I am emotionally tired and drained in the natural sense, yet I can do all in God's grace. I feel kind of numb right now. *"Move, Lord. Touch me in your power."*

In retrospect, I see I've been operating as if this race is a sprint, not a marathon. Having two to three daily meetings, etc. takes energy.

Monday, May 1.

New inmates poured into Bellwood today. All 60 bunks appear to be occupied. The new arrivals come from the other building where some had been sleeping on mattresses on the floor.

Two new fellows came to Bible study. One of them, Jeff, prayed during the altar call. I told the story of the Prodigal Son from Luke 15.

I rejoice over another soul coming home to the Father. Yet, knowing that I'm not as great a risk as some who have been released, I felt disappointed not to have been let out. Even some felons were to be released, along with misdemeanants.

After three months I'm ready for a change. I've been hoping for some type of dramatic release. But what is God's will?

"Jesus, I'm a skillet-headed, Tennessee boy. You often seem to need handwriting on the wall to reach me. Don't give up. Thanks for Your patience.

"Praise You—praise You—wondrous are You, precious Lord— high and mighty, glorious and lifted up above the heavenlies, Yeshua.

"Lord, give me abundant grace. Fill Mary and me with Your Spirit. Dare I ask for that when my flesh wants to be out of here? How about a chariot of fire to sweep me away from this place?"

Today is day 90 for me. Ninety exotic days in Bellwood Barracks.

My watch says 11:21 p.m. The deputy is late with the 11 o'clock head count. Most can't really get to sleep until afterwards.

I missed not having any visitors this Monday. A visitor breaks up the day and gets me out for a change of scenery, and a brief glimpse of God's majestic outdoors. And I still need and delight in those seasons of praise in the booth, during the visitation and after my visitor leaves.

I'm not complaining. I probably receive up to 75 percent of the total visitors received by the 60 men here. Certainly I get more mail than all combined. The fellows have never complained or mentioned this.

Even local family members don't visit the men as they should. Some here never have visitors! ". . . I was sick, and ye visited Me: I was in prison, and ye came unto Me" (Matthew 25:36).

Tuesday, May 2.

What a day! I was awakened at 1:10 this morning and told I was being transferred to a work camp.

I woke up Mark and transferred most of the song sheets, Bibles, and assorted literature, etc. to him. I laid hands on my co-teacher officially and spiritually, delegating Bellwood church responsibilities to him. I left about 3:30 a.m. and was totally processed out of the Fulton County Jail. They gave my personal property back, minus my shirt and pants and a few other items which couldn't be located.

After breakfast in a holding cell, 13 of us were driven by van to the new location around the corner. This is a county camp providing labor for road and trash details. I will have the opportunity to get outside during the day.

During the processing into the work camp we were kept in one holding cell for around four hours. I told my 12 cellmates about a man in the Bible—Joseph—who got framed and sent to prison. They listened quietly. I also explained why I was in jail. However, the excitement of this move was too much to hold their attention very long.

We got bologna and peanut butter and jelly sandwiches for lunch. We were issued white uniforms with a blue stripe down the leg, linens, and a toilet kit. Then we were taken to our barracks and given bunks and a required shower.

A lady officer in a brown uniform sat at a table as she oriented us: "You will meet first with your counselor on Thursday. You will have no visitors until then. Visitors' names must be on the list. This will take two or three days.

"You must earn everything here, including phone calls. You cannot use the phone until Friday."

My mind is spinning from this decided turn of events. They've taken me away from my precious Bellwood church. What does it all mean? Is this God's way of indicating that I am released from responsibilities to Bellwood?

Am I to be a jail-to-jail, spiritual Johnny Appleseed? My heart is in Bellwood. My reason for staying was the church there. Now suddenly that is taken from me. I feel robbed, yet relieved. Yet no church is owned by any pastor. It is Christ's body. Jesus is the only indispensable Shepherd.

Obviously a corner has been turned. It's big decision time again. That is on my mind today. What can I accomplish for the fellows in Bellwood by staying here? I feel released from the church. I have a peace about leaving that I did not have when wrestling with God back in February. There is a sense of completion, though an abrupt and surprising finish.

I will leave. Yes, that's what I will do. I can do no more for the Bellwood brothers from here. I can now help them more from the outside. Most all alums are already out.

But how to get out of this place? I was just told no phone calls until Friday, three days from now.

I've made the decision to go, but I'm incommunicado for three days. *"Make a way, Lord! I need to reach friends and ask that my appeal bond be paid."*

There are phones around, I'm told, but we are not to use them, and how would it look for a minister to be breaking rules? No, that's not of the Lord. I'll stay until I can use a phone with permission, even if I must wait until Friday.

I'm anxious to get out. It's like being ready to go home after the work week is over—and more. I don't like pointless delays. Or traffic jams. *"Lord, can You get me out of here today?"*

About four p.m. an officer walked into this barracks and started calling for someone. Over the noise it sounded like "care." Some pronounce my name that way. Some say "cur." I say "car." Did he mean me?

We sort of agreed that I fitted the bill, so without explanation he led me to the other end of the building where he said, "You have a visitor." How could this be? Visitors weren't supposed to be permitted until their names were listed. It wasn't Friday yet. And who even knew I was here?

Suddenly I saw the best sight I'd seen all day: Pastor Don Wade's beaming face. "As he's already here, go ahead and see him," the officer said cheerfully.

In the visitation booth Don explained, "I went to the other facility. They sent for you, then discovered you weren't there. Then they told me you were here. I thought I would take a chance and see if I could get in."

It was another one of those things that often "just happens" after you've prayed.

"Your coming is a specific answer to prayer," I told Don. "I've decided to leave. I can't help the Bellwood church from here. Nor can I minister much being on a work detail all day. Would you call and start the ball rolling?"

Don excitedly agreed. It was now after four p.m. We prayed and parted quickly. He sped away on his mission. *"Oh, thank You, Jesus."*

How powerful an answer this is to me. I see it as wonderful confirmation that leaving is God's will. I am relieved . . . jubilant . . . excited!

I returned to my barracks where I shook a few hands and distributed some Christian literature and showed my abortion pictures once more.

As I waited, I wondered: Can my friends be reached this late in the day? Will the office be closed soon, making release impossible this evening?

We ate around 5:30—spaghetti complete with a vegetable and salad bar. The food seemed better than at the other location. I guess outside workers need more food than idlers sitting in Bellwood.

Shortly after supper I was summoned to a very nice office where an important looking gentleman in civilian dress said, "I've been talking with the judge. You can be released if you're willing to sign the appeal bond. Is that agreeable?"

"Yes, it is."

"The bond is next door at the county jail. We'll take you over."

I packed up and was escorted back to the main building of the Fulton County Jail where I had been processed out this morning. I signed the bond before another important looking officer and was met by the smiling faces and hugs of friends Michael and Jane. Their familiar faces and warm words would make a sweet memory.

After signing, I told the county jail officer, "They didn't return my shirt or pants to me yesterday. I have no clothes to wear out except a sweater which was given back."

Evidently my shirt and pants had been misplaced or worse. I thought to myself, "If necessary, I could walk out in the sweater using the sleeves for pant legs."

The officer asked, "What size uniform do you wear?" When I said "medium," he disappeared. In a few moments he returned with a two-piece outfit like the one I had worn in Bellwood for three months.

He spoke in a gentle tone. "You can go in the Captain's office and put it on. It's empty." I was savoring each moment of this rapidly closing drama. It was like the final minutes of a big ball game when you know your team has it won. Spiritual victories had been won indeed, and I'm confident that time will reveal others as well.

I changed clothes and shook hands with the officer, saying goodby. As we walked out I spotted an officer friend sitting behind a table. Shaking his hand, I said, "See you, Sarge." He smiled back. A unique chapter was ending during which I've learned more about myself and ministry. A chapter in which I've made many new friends.

Another **Atlanta Journal and Constitution** reporter, Sandra McIntosh, and a photographer met me as I emerged. After the interview, Michael, Jane, and I sped away down the interstate. Spring had come since my entrance into Bellwood. The trees looked so very fresh and green.

May 2 began like most other days for Mary. After some intensive housecleaning, she finished writing her almost daily letter to me. Interestingly, her attention the day before had been drawn to Peter's miraculous release in Acts. She sensed something was up.

At 5:35 p.m. she got a call. When the phone rang, she had a thought she had not had: "Is this the call?"

"Mary, Fred has been released. Come as quickly as you can. He should be out within the hour . . . ."

"He's out! This is over! This is no time for losing control. I've got to drive to Atlanta."

She called her family. Her friend, Nancy Davis got a baby sitter so she could make the trip with Mary. The two climbed into our old van and Mary turned the key. The van knew right where to go. It had been keeping steady company with I-20 for several months.

I ended up in the home of friends near Atlanta. While we waited for Mary, my hostess said, "You can have anything you want to eat. Is your heart set on anything?"

Having had an early supper, I settled for popcorn. Finally, about mid-evening, we heard the roar of our old V-8. "There's Mary," my hostess exclaimed.

We hurried outside to meet them. My heart beat faster. How wonderful to see the godly wife who had walked through this adventure with me. I was so proud of her. She's spiritually tough. Her steadfastness, perseverance, moral support, and quiet peace helped me so much. Mary's a winner. I love her. Truly "a prudent wife is from the Lord" (Proverbs 19:14).

The greetings were long awaited and warm. Our group laughed and talked together.

Later, the numbers thinned as the hours disappeared. Sometime after midnight Mary and I wound down our talking in the den and also called it a day. What a day it had been.

Chapter 20

"Bellwood Follow-up"

Pastor Mark and I have continually corresponded since I left. This letter came from him, dated 7-5-89:

Dear Brother Fred:

Church is going along great. I'm really feeling good about eight new members. The guys are really hungry for the Word. We had another pro-life member [a rescuer], but he had only four days to serve.

We have service right after mornin' count time. I was feeling kind of bad sometime because they beat me to the tables in the morning. What I decided to do was put my Bible on a table and then run to the bathroom and wash and brush my teeth before they came.

One of the new members told me the other day at dinner that he is really getting something from the class. What I've been teaching lately, besides the prayer service, is on Proverbs, a chapter for each day of the month. The guys are really getting into the facts of each scripture, and they get real excited after they discover what they have just read and begin applying the scripture to their life.

Take care, Yours in Christ,

Mark

Mark and I talked and prayed on the phone again. Eleven are currently attending the Bible study. He's had some challenges to his authority. Disruptive inmates try to scare or discourage members away from the group. He's hanging in there. "Mark, I'm so proud of you," I told him. "Keep going."

Encouragement is so important, as I well know. On August 12, I wrote Mark a letter to read to the Bellwood church.

Dear Bellwood members:

Greetings and grace to you.

Please know that I think of the church and you members there every day. Even though I don't know all of you, I pray for you. God knows who you are. I am praying for God to be honored and respected in everything that happens there.

I hear some encouraging things about your hunger to grow and learn the precious Word of God. That's wonderful. I hear of your eagerness to attend the meetings and learn. That's a good sign.

I know Mark pretty well by now. I was there three months. I know that he cares for the Lord and you. I know that at one point this spring he was offered the chance to be a trustee and leave Bellwood. It was a good deal. He was very tempted to take it. But he is still there. He wants to serve and teach. His faithfulness to the Lord will be rewarded.

Colossians 1:28 says, "Whom we preach, warning every man, and teaching every man in all wisdom; that we may present every man perfect in Christ Jesus . . . . "

We see God's game plan in this verse. Preaching is first—telling people the wonderful wisdom and power of the precious Word of God and giving high priority to the saving blood of Jesus Christ.

For there to be preaching, there must be both a preacher and listeners willing to hear what is being taught. Colossians 1:28 goes on to say that warning every man is important. Why do we need to read or hear warnings from the Bible day after day?

A man may be trying to mix the teaching of Christ with strange doctrine. The cults confuse many with strange teachings. The Bible is our yardstick or plumb line to help us separate God's Word from man's opinion.

Sadly, some in prison or jail will not turn to God's Word. Warn the hardhearted. Pray for them.

Warning from God's Word is an evidence of God's love for us. Of Paul's love for us. Of Mark's love for you.

Finally, we see the goal of the Apostle Paul in this verse: "That we may present every man perfect in Christ Jesus." To be perfect means finished or mature. At about age 20, one is mature physically. When one is spiritually mature, he is well developed with spiritual muscles and endurance that he did not have yesterday.

One who plugs into teaching and abides in Christ and in the fellowship of a church shows a desire for this maturity. He's like a football player who comes to practice as opposed to one who doesn't come and give it all he's got.

I pray that every one of you goes on to become fully mature in Christ, even as you probably are already fully grown physically.

Remember that I am praying for you: *"Lord, I love You. I lift up Bellwood and Brother Mark and every man there to You right now. I ask for Your watchcare over them. Keep them from the Evil One. Give them the needed desire and discipline to study, grow, and seek after Jesus. Keep them from the traps and snares of worldliness.*

"Keep them close, dear Jesus. Show them the tricks and emptiness of the Devil's lures.

"Fill them with your Spirit. Save any that are not saved.

"Jesus, give Brother Mark wisdom and enabling as he leads the group day by day. I ask this all in the wonderful name of Jesus, Amen."

In Jesus' Love,'

Brother Fred Kerr

I had lunch in July with Keith, a brother who rededicated his life while in Bellwood. He sells cars. Keith took me to a nice seafood restaurant where he shared glowing stories of victories in his family, including an actual miracle in his wife's life.

Other Bellwood alums have called me and I have reached a few. I've learned of both victories and setbacks. Many are not like Keith. They can use a rigorous church discipleship program. Those addicted to alcohol and drugs really need a full year at a highly structured, Christian boot camp. They need relief from the temptations of the old, undisciplined life style. They need someone to stand with them day by day, as Jesus did with His twelve.

It is now mid-September, following my May release. Brother Mark has just "packed it up!" Charges against him were finally dropped as he hoped they would be. He had been in jail since last November. He also has wonderful stories to tell of God's workings and provision.

Mark phoned me after his release. We rejoiced and thanked God in prayer. Now he can resume his life and reopen his wholesale T-shirt printing operation again.

Upon leaving, Mark turned the Bellwood group over to a cheerful African fellow who was in the group when I was there. I pray for Victor's leadership and acceptance by the others. There is prejudice against many foreigners among the inmates. The Bellwood church has been going for eight months now. Lord willing, our paths will cross again.

Chapter 21

"God Meant It for Good"

As I am finalizing this manuscript, I see through my office window a lush, green fig tree which has provided us with tasty fruit this summer. Sipping a hot cup of Postum in relative comfort and freedom, I think back a few months ago to a different looking place where this journal began last February. I recall—and marvel over—the verse God gave me on the morning of the trial, "Wait for the Lord; Be strong, and let your heart take courage; Yes, wait for the Lord" (Psalm 27:14, NASV).

God kept His promise to me. He showed Himself to be faithful. I was not deserted. Exciting ministry opportunities occurred. It wasn't easy, but I don't regret it. I survived and thrived. Mary and I both agree that we are both stronger Christians for this experience.

What a faith-stretching time! I learned in a different way that wherever God sends, He supplies. The Lord doesn't lead His beloved children into tight spots and then abandon them.

I was stretched by being thrust into a concentrated, round-the-clock pastoral ministry to scores of men. And though not comparable to the hardship and suffering that many Christians in various countries face today, it was a growth experience for me. His grace was wonderfully adequate, as I asked Jesus to use me somehow each day.

According to the list I kept in my Bible, at least 60 men prayed the sinner's prayer with Mark or me. It's always affirming to find another situation where old fashioned, Biblical evangelism works as it has for centuries. God doesn't change. The basics don't either.

The experience also gave opportunities to tell and show inmates and officers what an abortion does to an innocent child. Reality dawned on many. Shackles of ignorance were broken.

By faith, I believe that many unborn will be spared the abortionists' knives and suction deaths because of Brenda's and my opportunities to expose people to the truth about baby killing.

God will not be mocked. His side wins. Evil loses. The only question is when.

God blessed in the natural as well. Though I haven't reached the goal yet, my cholesterol level dropped significantly over the three months. It's the "Bellwood pro-life diet."

I give God every ounce of the glory for whatever happened in Bellwood. I definitely did not want to go there, or stay for three months. The Lord twisted my arm. When I arrive in Heaven, I'll be curious to discover all that really took place.

"Praise You, Jesus! Thank You, Lord of mercy, forgiveness, and salvation. I acknowledge that You alone are worthy of doing great things. I don't want to withhold any of the honor due You for your mighty working in all this. To You alone belongs all the praise and glory. You alone can redeem. You alone can transform a blackened heart to one as white as snow. I bow before You, wonderful Father. Great is Jehovah. Hallelujah!"

"A Special Invitation"

In these final pages, I address you, my reader.

Do you have the peace and joy you want? Is something missing deep down inside? Do you want release from the prison house of sin? Do you know which way you would go if you died tonight?

If not, you can know the certainty of eternal life, even as I do today. Jesus wants you to know. He wants to come in and take control of your life? Do you want that? Will you let Him do so? If so, you can kneel right now and simply tell Jesus:

"Dear Lord Jesus, I am a sinner. I am sorry for my sins. I believe that You died on the cross to pay for all my sins. Right now I invite You to come into my heart and sit on the throne of my life.

"From this moment on You are my Lord and my Savior. I will do whatever You tell me to do. I am depending completely on You to fill me with Your spirit, give me direction, and take me to heaven when my time comes. Thank You, Lord, for the free gift of eternal life which you have given me. In Jesus' name, Amen."

Here are seven essential principles which I urge you to follow in your walk as a new believer:

1. Stand firmly on promises from the Bible that give a believer the assurance of eternal life. Repeat them aloud as often as doubts attack you. Look up—even memorize John 5:24, 6:37, 10:28; Romans 10:13; 1 John 5:12, 13.

2. Read your Bible every day to get to know Jesus better and His will for your life (Psalm 1:2, 119:9, 11).

3. Talk daily to Jesus, your new Master and Friend (Mark 1:35; Psalm 27:7, 8).

4. Tell others what Christ has done in your life and what He can do in theirs. Start today giving your testimony (Luke 8:38, 39; Mark 16:15).

5. Get into a Bible-believing, Christ-proclaiming church for corporate worship, prayer, fellowship, and Scriptural teaching (Hebrews 10:25, Acts 2:42-47).

6. Separate yourself from the old life of impurity, sin, and worldliness. Stay clear of sin's old hangouts, play toys, and those who would pull you back into the old ways (2 Corinthians 6:14-17).

7. Determine to walk by faith and dependence on the inexhaustible resources of God. But remember, we need not be great men and women of God, but only men and women of a great God. "Not that I have great faith," said Hudson Taylor, "but that He is faithful."

You may think, "Lord, who am I? I can't do much." That's great! God is only looking for a lamp cord, not a power source.

If you have just prayed and invited Jesus Christ the Lord to come and take over your life, I'd like to know! Please write me today at the address below.

Fred Kerr
c/o Hannibal Books
31 Holiday Drive
Hannibal, MO 63401

I may also be contacted at this address for
speaking engagements.

Resources for Pro-lifers:

Americans Against Abortion, Box 70, Lindale, TX 75771, offers powerful brochures.

American Portrait Films, 1695 W. Crescent Avenue, Suite 500, Anaheim, CA 92801, produces and distributes conscience-awakening films, including, "The Silent Scream," "A Matter of Choice," and "Conceived in Liberty."

Birthright, 777 Coxwell Avenue, Toronto, Canada, M4C-3C6 1-800-328-LOVE, Operates nearly 600 crisis pregnancy centers in the United States and Canada.

Bethany Christian Services, 901 Eastern Ave. NE, Grand Rapids, MI 49503, 616-459-6273 (office), 1-800-238-4269 (hotline), is an evangelical adoption agency.

Christian Life Commission of the Southern Baptist Convention, 901 Commerce Street, Suite 550, Nashville, TN 37203, offers a number of inexpensive, well-written, Biblically-fortressed booklets on abortion and pro-life concerns.

Christian Maternity Home Association, c/o Loving and Caring, 1817 Olde Homestead Lane, Suite H, Lancaster, PA 17601, 717-293-3230, helps groups start maternity homes, writes state licensing manuals, helps train staff, provides consultation and program review, and publishes an annual directory.

Focus on the Family, Pomona, CA 91799, has a wealth of family-related resources with a pro-life emphasis, including Focus on the Family Citizen (one-year membership $15) and Focus on the Family Physician (one-year membership $20.)

Hannibal Books, 31 Holiday Drive, Hannibal, MO 63401, a Christian publishing house with a strong pro-life stance, will shortly have available, in addition to *90 Days for Life,* a challenging new book, *We Can Change America . . . and Here's How* by Darylann Whitemarsh, an outstanding Christian political activist. See the order form at the end of this book.

Hayes Publishing Co., Inc., 6304 Hamilton Avenue, Cincinnati, Ohio 45234, publishes graphic leaflets, brochures, cassettes, and slide presentations.

Home Mission Board, Southern Baptist Convention, 1350 Spring Street, N.W., Atlanta, GA 30367, sponsors the Sellers Baptist Home and Adoption Center in New Orleans, LA, for maternity clients. Pregnant women may call a toll-free number, 1-800-962-0851, for referral to local churches and contact persons for counseling.

Intercessors for America, P.O. Box 2639, Reston, VA 22090, is publisher of the influential booklets "Abortion in America" and "When You Were Formed in Secret."

Liberty Godparent Ministries, PO Box 27000, Lynchburg, VA 24506, 804-384-3043 (office), 1-800-368-3336 (hotline), offers special assistance.

Loving and Caring, Inc., 1817 Homestead Lane, Lancaster, PA 17601, 717-293-3230, trains host couples for women with crisis pregnancies, offers counseling, retreats and seminars, and publishes counseling materials.

National Right to Life Educational Trust Fund, 419 7th Street, NW., Suite 500, Washington, DC.C. 20004 offers a wide variety of pro-life materials and brochures.

New Beginnings, 40 25th Avenue North, St. Cloud, MN 56303, 612-255-1252, sponsors a home for single pregnant women, and a self-help program providing professional counseling and support services.

Operation Rescue, P.O. Box 1180, Binghamton, NY 13902 offers a variety of video and audio cassettes, and literature. The story of Operation Rescue, published under that title by Whitaker House, by Randall A. Terry, may be purchased at your local Christian book store, or from Operation Rescue.

Acknowledgements & Appreciations

I wish to express deep appreciation to my wife Mary for her support and help with material ideas, wording, proof reading, correspondence, and a myriad of other details relating to this book.

Special thanks goes to Mary Em Hobbs for the idea of keeping a journal, and later encouraging me to make it into a book. As with most first drafts, the original journal material needed refinement for readability and completeness. However, I have made every effort to preserve the original flavor and diversity which the journal style affords.

I wish to further thank,

Dr. Richard Belcher for encouragement and insights into the world of publishing.

Jan Surratt for giving helpful advice on the manuscript.

William "Sonny" Billingsley and Johnny Humphries for help with photography.

Our numerous friends for the support Mary and I were given in many ways.

Janet Bates and Roberta Beaty for helpful comments and proof reading.

Numerous others for personal words of encouragement.

ADDITIONAL BOOKS AVAILABLE
FROM HANNIBAL BOOKS
Please send me . . . .

90 Days for Life by Fred Kerr. An important document in the pro-life movement.

_____ Copies at $7.95 = _____

Where Is God When a Child Suffers? by Penny Giesbrecht. How a Christian family copes with their child's pain in the light of God's love.

_____ Copies at $8.95 = _____

What Are They Teaching Our Children? by Mel and Norma Gabler. Documentation that shows how America's moral and religious heritage has been stripped from many public school textbooks.

_____ Copies at $5.95 = _____

The Greatest Book Ever Written by Dr. Rochunga Pudaite with James C. Hefley, Ph.D. Praised by evangelical leaders as an outstanding apologetic on the Bible.

_____ Copies at $9.95 = _____

COMING SOON
FROM HANNIBAL BOOKS

We Can Change America . . . and Here's How" by Darylann Whitemarsh. How to make things happen in the public arena. Especially helpful for pro-lifers to use in coming battles to save the unborn.

_____ Copies at $9.95 = _____

Guilty Until Proven Innocent by Keith Barnhart with Lila Shelburne. Dramatic true story of the prosecution of an innocent pastor charged with sexual child abuse. A must book for all who work with children.

_____ Copies at $9.95 = _____

Please add $2.00 postage and handling for first book, plus .50 for each additional book.

Shipping & Handling _____

MO residents add sales tax _____

TOTAL ENCLOSED (Check or money order) _____

Name _____

Address _____

City _____ State _____ Zip _____ Phone _____